The
FOOTBALL
FANBOOK

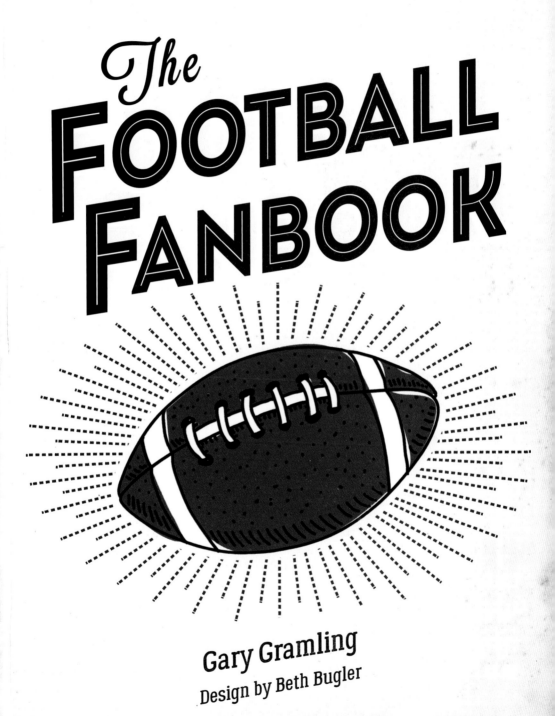

Gary Gramling

Design by Beth Bugler

Denver Broncos fans, Sports Authority Field at Mile High

Writer: Gary Gramling
Designer: Beth Bugler
Editor: Elizabeth McGarr McCue
Copy Editor: Pamela Roberts
Reporter: Jeremy Fuchs
Illustrator: Colin Hayes
Production Manager: Hillary Leary

ISBN: 978-1-68330-007-6
Library of Congress Control Number: 2017934909

First edition, 2017

1 QGT 17

10 9 8 7 6 5 4 3 2 1

We welcome your comments and suggestions
about Time Inc. Books. Please write to us at:

Time Inc. Books
Attention: Book Editors
P.O. Box 62310
Tampa, FL 33662-2310
(800) 765-6400

timeincbooks.com

Time Inc. Books products may be purchased for
business or promotional use. For information on bulk
purchases, please contact Christi Crowley in the
Special Sales Department at (845) 895-9858.

CONTENTS

KICKOFF

When I was very young, we had an autumn Sunday tradition at the King house in northern Connecticut: up early, church, leaf-raking . . . and then, always, the Giants game on TV at 1 p.m. At the end of the game, the three boys and my father would go out to the yard and throw the football around. I have such great memories of those Sundays. I am amazed, today, thinking about my good fortune in life. Now I get to watch games for a living, and I get to learn about football from the smartest people who play and coach the sport.

King with former Colts QB Peyton Manning in 2007.

I will give you an example. After Super Bowl LI, I had the chance to sit with quarterback Tom Brady and spend more than an hour with him talking about the greatest comeback in Super Bowl history, his Patriots' victory over the Falcons. He explained so much about each individual big play in the win. I felt as if I were in the huddle right next to receiver Julian Edelman. That is the kind of information I wish I had when I was watching games with my family. Football is so complex. It's cool to have a great player sit down and explain the complicated parts of an important game in such detail.

I never had a book like the one you have in your hands right now, a guide to tell you why and how things happen in this drama with 22 people fighting for field

position on every play. All 22 have jobs to do. But do you really know what the guard is supposed to do when the quarterback goes back to pass? And do you know why that guard's assignment is different from what the others on the line have to do? This book is the perfect tool to understand how the game works—and I guarantee you that you'll be a smarter fan after reading this. It's the next best thing to sitting down with Tom Brady and listening to him tell you how he helped his team win that Super Bowl. It's the kind of book I wish I had when I was your age. Happy reading.

Peter King

Editor-in-chief, The MMQB, and
SPORTS ILLUSTRATED *NFL expert*

PETER KING'S FIVE FAVORITE THINGS ABOUT FOOTBALL

1. I love never—and I mean never—knowing who's going to win when the game starts. Drama is fun.

2. I love fall Sunday afternoons, especially when the games begin to mean so much in November.

3. I love games that are tied late in the fourth quarter.

4. I love when new stars are born, which happens every year in the NFL.

5. I love writing about things no one else sees or experiences when it comes to the most popular sport in America.

WELCOME TO

PERFECTVILLE

POP. 1

FOUNDED 1972

Chapter

1

KNOW THESE NUMBERS

Don't let anybody tell you that
the only numbers that matter
are the ones on the scoreboard.
These are the stats and figures
that every NFL fan should
know by heart.

MOST SUPER BOWL TITLES WON BY A PLAYER

TIE

5

Tom Brady

2000–2016

Charles Haley

1986–1999

CHARLES HALEY

Tom Brady had a record night on February 5, 2017. When the Patriots' legend took the field for Super Bowl LI, he became the first player in NFL history to appear in seven Super Bowls. He then proceeded to throw for a Super Bowl–record 466 yards on a record 43 pass completions. It was all part of leading New England back from a 25-point deficit against the Falcons in a game the Patriots won 34–28. The Pats had the biggest comeback in Super Bowl history in the first Super Bowl to go into overtime. Brady left the field that night with his fifth victory in the big game.

Of course, that fifth championship only ties a record. Brady shares it with Hall of Fame pass rusher Charles Haley. Haley led the 49ers (Super Bowls XXIII and XXIV) and the Cowboys (XXVII and XXVIII) to back-to-back titles. When he helped Dallas topple the Steelers in Super Bowl XXX, he became the first to get "one for the thumb," 21 years before Brady got his fifth.

Some of Brady's Most Impressive Records*

208
Most wins (regular season and playoffs) by a starting QB

10
Most consecutive postseason wins by a QB

9,094
Most career passing yards in the playoffs

20
Most pass completions in the first half of a Super Bowl

*All stats through Super Bowl LI

MOST WINS BY A HEAD COACH

328 — Don Shula

1963–1995

Don Shula has more wins than any head coach in NFL history because he coached for a really long time. But he also has the most wins because he won more than two-thirds of his games! Shula had only two losing seasons in his 33 years of coaching, for the Baltimore Colts and then the Dolphins. In 1972, he led Miami to the only perfect season in the Super Bowl era and won the big game again a year later. His .677 career winning percentage is the 10th highest of all time.

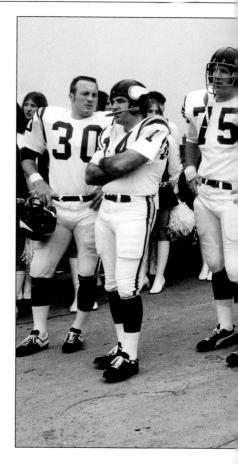

MOST SUPER BOWL TITLES WON BY A TEAM

6 — Pittsburgh Steelers

The Lombardi Trophy isn't made out of steel, but it might as well be. The Steelers own six of these beauties. They've been to the Super Bowl eight times, tied for second most behind the Patriots.

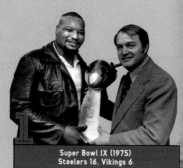

Super Bowl IX (1975)
Steelers 16, Vikings 6

2	**3**	**4**	**5**	**6**
Super Bowl X (1976) Steelers 21, Cowboys 17	Super Bowl XIII (1979) Steelers 35, Cowboys 31	Super Bowl XIV (1980) Steelers 31, Rams 19	Super Bowl XL (2006) Steelers 21, Seahawks 10	Super Bowl XLIII (2009) Steelers 27, Cardinals 23

MOST CAREER TOUCHDOWNS

208 Jerry Rice
1985–2004

During the 2016 NFL season, Cardinals star receiver Larry Fitzgerald became the 24th player in league history to score 100 touchdowns in his career. Really impressive, right? It is . . . until you consider that legendary wide receiver Jerry Rice scored twice as many during his magnificent career. Rice has a handful of NFL records, but the most impressive mark he owns is this one. He was the focal point of the 49ers' nearly unstoppable West Coast offense in the 1980s and 1990s. And he was the first wide receiver in more than 90 years to play past his 40th birthday. (He scored 10 of his TDs after turning 40.) During the 2000s, it looked as if running back LaDainian Tomlinson might make a go at reaching 208. But his career ended with a three-TD season in 2011, leaving him 46 short of Rice. Randy Moss, who holds the single-season receiving record of 23 TDs, scored 51 fewer career touchdowns than Rice. Emmitt Smith, football's all-time leading rusher who was known for his smooth moves and long playing career, came up 33 TDs short.

Close? Not really....

2.	Emmitt Smith	175	1990–2004
3.	LaDainian Tomlinson	162	2001–2011
4.	Randy Moss	157	1998–2012
5.	Terrell Owens	156	1996–2010
6.	Marcus Allen	145	1982–1997
7.	Marshall Faulk	136	1994–2005
8.	Cris Carter	131	1987–2002
9.	Marvin Harrison	128	1996–2008
10.	Jim Brown	126	1957–1965
11.	Walter Payton	125	1975–1987

MOST CAREER TOUCHDOWN PASSES

Peyton Manning

1998–2015

Quarterbacking in the NFL wasn't always easy for Peyton Manning. Rewind to his rookie year, in 1998—his first season after graduating from the University of Tennessee. In his NFL debut, Manning threw three interceptions. In fact, the first time one of his passes ever went for a touchdown in the NFL was when it was thrown to the wrong team. (Dolphins defensive back Terrell Buckley intercepted Manning and returned the pick for a touchdown in that first game.) The quarterback went on to throw a whopping 28 interceptions as a rookie (a QB has thrown that many picks in a year only 18 times in NFL history), and his Colts went 3–13, tying for the league's worst record. Of course, things got better. As he mastered running an NFL offense and learned to toy with opposing defenses, Manning went on to become one of the greatest players in league history. He retired after helping the Broncos to a victory in Super Bowl 50 at the end of the 2016 season. That year he threw touchdown pass number 539 (to tight end Owen Daniels). Manning retired with 31 more TD passes than Packers QB Brett Favre, who is second on the all-time list. No other quarterback has ever thrown 500 in a career.

Peyton's Place in History

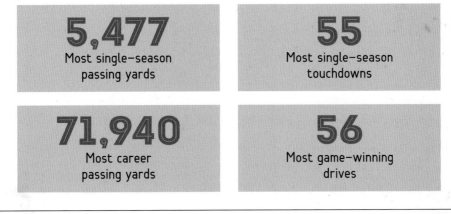

5,477
Most single-season
passing yards

55
Most single-season
touchdowns

71,940
Most career
passing yards

56
Most game-winning
drives

MOST CAREER RUSHING YARDS

18,355

Emmitt Smith
1990–2004

The modern NFL offense is all about throwing the pigskin. But there was a time when most teams moved the ball on the ground, and there was nothing more valuable to a team than having a star running back. For the great Dallas Cowboys teams of the 1990s, Emmitt Smith was that player. He broke into the league as a shifty runner who packed a wallop. But it was his outstanding instincts and high football IQ that allowed him to thrive even after he was no longer a physical freak. Smith rushed for 1,000 yards in a season 11 times, and he finished his career atop the all-time list, more than 1,600 yards ahead of the previous leader, Walter Payton.

MOST RUSHING YARDS IN A SEASON

Eric Dickerson

Los Angeles Rams, 1984

When Eric Dickerson had his record-setting year, he became only the second player in NFL history to rush for 2,000 yards in a season. Since then, five more runners have joined the 2,000-yard club, forcing Dickerson to sweat it out on the last week of those seasons. In 2012, Adrian Peterson came up eight yards short of the mark. Dickerson's record has stood for more than 30 years, and with teams leaning more toward the passing game, it could stand much longer.

MOST RUSHING YARDS IN A GAME

296 — Adrian Peterson

Chargers vs. Vikings, November 4, 2007

At the end of the first half of this game between San Diego and Minnesota, history was made. Chargers defensive back Antonio Cromartie caught a missed field goal at the back of the end zone and returned it for a touchdown, the NFL's first 109-yard play. And yet, Cromartie's was only the second most prominent record set that day. Adrian Peterson, the Vikings' star rookie running back, proved to be positively unstoppable. His second-half TD dashes of 64 and 46 yards helped him run into the history books as well. A three-yard rush late in the fourth quarter of a 35–17 victory sent Peterson past the previous single-game rushing record of 295, held by Jamal Lewis.

MOST RECEIVING YARDS IN ONE GAME

336

Flipper Anderson

Rams vs. Saints,
November 26, 1989

Willie (Flipper) Anderson was known for big plays. He's one of only six players in NFL history to average more than 20 yards per catch on more than 200 receptions. And the biggest game of his life—or any receiver's, as it turned out—came midway through the 1989 season, when he caught 15 passes and racked up more receiving yards than any player had in a single game.

LONGEST PLAY IN NFL HISTORY

109 YARDS

TIE

Cordarrelle Patterson

Packers vs. Vikings, October 27, 2013

Antonio Cromartie

Chargers vs. Vikings, November 4, 2007

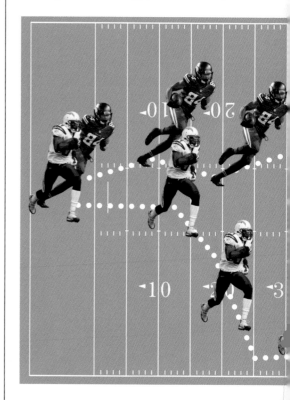

There are records that are thought to be unbreakable, and then there are records that are literally unbreakable. And unless there's a rule change that makes a football field longer, the record for longest play in NFL history can never be broken; it can only be tied. Antonio Cromartie set it first. With opposing Minnesota attempting a long field goal at the end of the first half, Cromartie waited in the end zone in case the kick fell short. It did, and he reached just over the end line to catch it. Then he took off, cutting up the right sideline and cruising past would-be tacklers untouched. In Patterson's case, he was running back a kick, an opening kickoff against rival Green Bay. He caught the ball with his back foot just in front of the end line, then darted and dodged through tacklers in the middle of the field. Once in the open, he headed for the left sideline and simply outran the kicker for the touchdown.

PERFECT RECORD

1972 Miami Dolphins

Rumor has it that every year, members of the 1972 Dolphins get together to celebrate when the NFL's last undefeated team loses a game. Such a loss has happened every season since, leaving the Dolphins as the only perfect team in the Super Bowl era. Yet the Dolphins don't always get the respect you would think they deserve. Many point to the schedule. Nowadays, the NFL uses a scheduling setup that ensures that every first-place team will face two teams that finished atop their divisions the previous season in addition to two other entire divisions. In 1972, the schedule was a simple rotation from year to year. The Dolphins faced only two teams that finished with winning records all regular season. (And those teams, the Chiefs and the Giants, both finished just 8–6.) However, a scheduling quirk forced the Dolphins to play the AFC championship game on the road, at Pittsburgh, a game they won 21–17. And the Dolphins nearly shut out the Washington Redskins in Super Bowl VII. Miami won 14–7; the only points Washington scored came on a freak play, on which a blocked field goal was scooped up by Dolphins kicker Garo Yepremian. He tried to throw a pass but accidentally flipped the ball backward behind his head, then deflected it forward to a defender, who ran it back for a touchdown.

Almost Perfect

These are the teams that made those Dolphins sweat it out for the longest.

YEAR	TEAM	WINS BEFORE FIRST LOSS	FINAL RECORD
2007	New England Patriots	18	18–1
2015	Carolina Panthers	14	17–2
1998	Denver Broncos	13	17–2
2005	Indianapolis Colts	13	14–3

MOST RECEPTIONS IN ONE GAME

21 Brandon Marshall

Broncos vs. Colts, December 13, 2009

MOST RECEPTIONS IN ONE SEASON

143   Marvin Harrison

Indianapolis Colts, 2002

Peyton Manning owns so many NFL passing records that it seems only natural that his favorite target would own one of football's most famous receiving marks. Marvin Harrison caught more passes from Manning than anyone else, and a whole lot of them came during the 2002 season. Weirdly enough, Harrison began that season with one of his worst games as a pro; he had just four catches in a victory over the Jaguars. But he caught 11 against the Dolphins one week later, and from then on he started hauling in receptions in bunches. He had double-digit catches in six games that season, including a whopping 14 in a November victory over the Cowboys. He set the single-season record for catches at Cleveland in mid-December—and there were still two games left in the season. By the time it was all over, Harrison had caught 20 more passes than anyone ever had in a year.

Brandon Marshall must have worn out his gloves against the Colts that day. He became only the second player in NFL history to have 20 or more catches in a single game. With his 21st reception he surpassed the previous record (20, by Terrell Owens in 2000). But this wasn't completely new territory for Marshall. He had 18 catches against the Chargers the previous season, a number that is still tied for the third-most catches in a game.

MOST SACKS IN A SEASON

Michael Strahan

New York Giants, 2001

You might know Michael Strahan as the goofy, gap-toothed TV host. Most of the quarterbacks who faced him in 2001, however, knew him as a walking nightmare. The speedy edge rusher had a record 22½ sacks that season, though the record isn't without controversy. The previous record (set by Mark Gastineau in 1984) was 22, and Strahan was stuck on 21½ until the final drive of the season. With the game out of reach, Packers QB Brett Favre seemed to intentionally fall into Strahan for the record-breaking sack. And, of course, the NFL didn't begin officially keeping track of the stat until 1982.

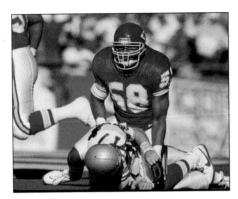

MOST SACKS IN A GAME

7 Derrick Thomas

Seahawks vs. Chiefs, November 11, 1990

Derrick Thomas had one of the most dominant games any player has ever had. Yet all the linebacker could think about afterward was the play that got away. After taking down Seattle QB Dave Krieg a record seven times, Thomas had Krieg in his sights for number 8 as time expired. But Krieg managed to break out of Thomas's clutches, then launch a game-winning touchdown to lead the Seahawks past Thomas and Kansas City 17–16. "I thought I had him," Thomas told reporters after the game. "He just stumbled back and caught his balance and threw the pass. That last sack I didn't get is the one I'm going to remember."

SINGLE–SEASON RECORD FOR BEING SACKED

76 David Carr

Houston Texans, 2002

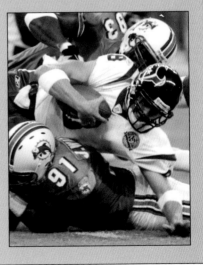

Being the first pick of the draft usually involves fame and glory. For David Carr, it involved a lot of ice packs. In their first-ever season, the expansion Texans didn't have much of an offensive line, and it showed. Carr was sacked more times than any quarterback in NFL history.

MOST CONSECUTIVE GAMES STARTED

297 Brett Favre

Green Bay Packers, September 27, 1992–
Minnesota Vikings, December 5, 2010

Back in Week 2 of the 1992 season, 22-year-old Brett Favre came off the bench for Green Bay and led the Pack to a dramatic victory over the Bengals, throwing a game-winning touchdown with 13 seconds left. Favre made his first career start one week later. Then he made every start for the Packers for nearly 16 years. Favre's streak extended to his one season with the Jets, then most of his two years with the Vikings. The streak finally ended when he suffered a major shoulder injury in 2010, at 41 years old. The streak is the longest ever for a nonspecialist.

Of all the great players to step foot on an NFL field, no one ever accounted for more points than a left-footed kicker from Denmark. Morten Andersen first came to the United States as a high school exchange student in 1977. He tried out for the football team and was so effective as a kicker that Michigan State University offered him a scholarship despite his lone season of football experience. The Saints' fourth-round pick in 1982 went on to become one of the most reliable kickers in NFL history. He made the Pro Bowl seven times and was so good for so long that he was named to the NFL's All-Decade teams for the 1980s and the 1990s. In his final game, in 2007, a 47-year-old Andersen made all three of the field goals he attempted and all five of his extra points to help the Falcons edge the Seahawks. He scored more points, kicked more field goals (565), and appeared in more games (382) than any other player in NFL history.

MOST CAREER POINTS

2,544

Morten Andersen

New Orleans Saints, 1982–1994; Atlanta Falcons, 1995–2000, 2006–2007; New York Giants, 2001; Kansas City Chiefs, 2002–2003; Minnesota Vikings, 2004

MOST CONSECUTIVE LOSSES

26 Tampa Bay Buccaneers

1976–1977

It's not easy being orange. Or at least it wasn't for the expansion Tampa Bay Buccaneers in 1976 and 1977. The Bucs went 0–14 in their inaugural season, the first team to ever play a 14-game season and not get a win or a tie. The next season, they lost their first 12 games. Coach John McKay *(left)* kept his sense of humor. After one game, he remarked, "We didn't tackle well today, but we made up for it by not blocking." The Bucs finally got their first win in franchise history the second-to-last game of the 1977 season, in New Orleans. One week later they defeated the St. Louis Cardinals to finish the season on a winning streak!

LONGEST FIELD GOAL

Kickers don't always get a lot of credit when they make kicks, and they shoulder all the blame when they miss. In 2013, Denver kicker Matt Prater earned some respect during a

HIGHEST SINGLE-SEASON PASSER RATING

122.5

Aaron Rodgers

Green Bay Packers, 2011

This is one record that requires quite a bit of math to explain. The NFL's passer rating formula (which differs from the one used in college) factors completion percentage, yards per pass attempt, touchdowns, and interceptions when measuring a passer's efficiency. According to all that math, no one was ever more efficient than Packers quarterback Aaron Rodgers in 2011, when he completed 68.3% of his passes for 9.25 yards per attempt, with 45 TDs and only six interceptions.

64 YARDS

Matt Prater

Titans vs. Broncos, December 8, 2013

late-season game when he got his Broncos three unexpected points. As time expired in the first half, Prater booted a 64-yard kick through Denver's thin air. The length of that field goal broke a record set by Saints kicker Tom Dempsey in 1970 and matched by three other kickers.

MOST TOUCHDOWNS IN A SEASON

LaDainian Tomlinson

San Diego Chargers, 2006

No one has visited the end zone in a single season as often as LaDainian Tomlinson did in 2006. And most of those touchdowns came between Week 6 and Week 15. Over those 10 games, the 27-year-old Tomlinson scored a ridiculous 28 times.

MOST TOUCHDOWN RECEPTIONS IN A SEASON

23 — Randy Moss

New England Patriots, 2007

Randy Moss was supposedly washed up when he joined the Patriots before the 2007 season. He was 30 years old, and he was coming off the worst statistical season of his career (42 catches, 553 yards, and three touchdowns for the Oakland Raiders). But a great receiver can only do so much with the wrong quarterback. Teamed up with all-time great Tom Brady in New England, Moss toyed with defensive backs all season long. Moss scored a touchdown in 13 of New England's 16 games that season and scored multiple touchdowns in half of their games that year. Not bad, considering he had scored 24 touchdowns in the previous three seasons combined!

MOST INTERCEPTIONS IN A SEASON

Dick (Night Train) Lane

Los Angeles Rams, 1952

Going into the 1952 season, opposing quarterbacks perhaps didn't know a lot about Rams rookie Dick Lane. It didn't take long for the league to learn all about Night Train, though. In his first season of pro football, Lane picked off an impressive 14 passes, a record that still stands more than 60 years later. He also came up with 298 interception return yards that year, the seventh most ever in a season. Apparently teams didn't learn to stop throwing at Lane. Two seasons later, Night Train had 10 interceptions.

OBSCURE FACTS

If you want to impress your friends with your sports knowledge, sometimes you have to dig a little deeper. Let us help: Here's a list of some of the coolest little-known football facts.

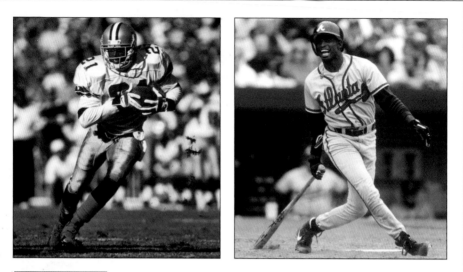

DUAL THREAT **DEION SANDERS IS THE ONLY ATHLETE TO PLAY IN A SUPER BOWL AND A WORLD SERIES.**

Sometimes he went by Prime Time, and other times he was Neon Deion. Regardless, there were enough nicknames for Deion Sanders to spread across both sports he played professionally. Arguably the greatest cover cornerback of all time, Sanders helped the 49ers win Super Bowl XXIX and the Cowboys win Super Bowl XXX. Playing in those games added to Sanders's impressive list of two-sport feats: Despite a broken foot, he batted second for the Atlanta Braves in four games of the 1992 World Series—and posted a .533 batting average!

Check out his résumé:

NFL	MLB
Baltimore Ravens (2004–2005)	Cincinnati Reds (1997, 2001)
Washington Redskins (2000)	San Francisco Giants (1995)
Dallas Cowboys (1995–1999)	Cincinnati Reds (1994–1995)
San Francisco 49ers (1994)	Atlanta Braves (1991–1994)
Atlanta Falcons (1989–1993)	New York Yankees (1989–1990)

#WINNING OTTO GRAHAM HAS THE HIGHEST WINNING PERCENTAGE OF ANY QUARTERBACK IN NFL HISTORY.

And you thought the Browns had a history of *losing* games. Otto Graham, the franchise's first quarterback, played 10 seasons and led Cleveland to the championship game in every year he played. The Browns won seven total AAFC and NFL titles. Graham won 81.4% of his games, the highest rate for any QB.

ABOUT THAT BALL

IT TAKES ABOUT 12 COWS TO SUPPLY THE NFL WITH ENOUGH LEATHER FOR SUPER BOWL FOOTBALLS.

You might call it a pigskin, but the Wilson Sporting Goods company makes NFL footballs out of cowhide. Wilson makes about 10 footballs from each cowhide. At the Super Bowl, each team gets 108 footballs (54 for practice, 54 for the game), plus there are 12 balls used for kicking. That means it takes about 12 cows to produce the 120 footballs needed for the Super Bowl.

EACH NFL FOOTBALL IS INSCRIBED WITH THE NICKNAME THE DUKE.

A close look at an official NFL game ball will reveal the NFL shield, the signature of the commissioner (currently Roger Goodell), the logo for Wilson (the company that produces the footballs), and the words THE DUKE. It's a nickname for the ball, and it's in honor of the man originally known as the Duke, longtime Giants owner Wellington Mara. (He was named after the Duke of Wellington.) Mara's father, Tim Mara, had arranged the contract with Wilson, and owners agreed to nickname the ball in his son's honor. So THE DUKE was inscribed on balls in the 1940s, 1950s, and 1960s, and again since the 2006 season began.

SINCE 1955, EVERY NFL FOOTBALL HAS BEEN MADE AT WILSON'S 150-PERSON FACTORY.

You might never have heard of Ada, Ohio, a small town with a population of fewer than 6,000 people. But it's home to the factory where every NFL football has been made for more than 60 years. Each ball is made of four panels and a single lace, with the lace threaded through 16 holes on each ball.

SOME NFL GAMES USED TO BE PLAYED WITH A WHITE BALL.

In 1929, the Providence Steam Rollers and the Chicago Cardinals met for a game under the lights. Because the lights weren't that reliable back then, the teams played with a white football to help with visibility. Players complained that the balls blended into white and lighter uniforms, and that the white footballs were too slick. But they were used on and off until the 1956 season.

FORMER VIKINGS KICKER FRED COX INVENTED THE NERF FOOTBALL.

In 1972, Fred Cox came up with the idea for a kicking game for kids that involved a foam-rubber ball. Parker Brothers didn't like the game idea but loved the ball itself, and the Nerf football was born.

HOPE SINCE THE NFL EXPANDED TO 32 TEAMS, AT LEAST ONE TEAM HAS GONE FROM LAST PLACE TO FIRST IN ITS DIVISION IN EVERY SEASON BUT ONE.

The NFL prides itself on parity: the concept that any team can be a winner during any season. And since the Texans entered the league as the 32nd franchise in 2002, that notion has been true for the most part. From 2002 through 2016—due in part to scheduling rules that give easier paths to teams with poor records the previous season—at least one team has made the leap from last place to first in its division, with the exception of the 2014 season. The 2009 Saints are the only team during the era to finish last place in their division one year, then win the Super Bowl the next season.

Biggest One-Season Improvement

Of all the quick turnarounds in NFL history, no team has had bigger one-year improvements than the Colts (from 1998 to 1999) or the Dolphins (from 2007 to 2008). For Indy, it wasn't completely unexpected. The Colts had tossed rookie QB Peyton Manning into the fire in 1998. He threw a league-high 28 interceptions, and the Colts won just three games. But the next season, Manning threw for more than 4,000 yards and cut his interception total to 15. And he got some help from a new star in the backfield, Edgerrin James *(below)*, who rushed for more than 1,500 yards. Indianapolis ended up winning 13 games in 1999. The 2008 Dolphins also won 10 games more than their 2007 counterparts, thanks largely to their use of the Wildcat formation, which often put two running backs on the field and no QB.

CHA–CHING

METLIFE STADIUM IS THE MOST EXPENSIVE STADIUM OF ALL TIME.

Considering it houses *both* the Giants and the Jets in East Rutherford, New Jersey, perhaps that's not as crazy as it seems. MetLife opened in 2010 and cost a whopping $1.6 billion to build.

THAT'S ME ## THE HEISMAN TROPHY WAS MODELED AFTER ED SMITH.

College football's most famous award is named after John Heisman. But the actual trophy was modeled after Ed Smith, a New York University running back in the 1930s.

THE HEISMAN MEMORIAL TROPHY
PRESENTED BY
THE HEISMAN TROPHY TRUST
TO
MARK INGRAM
UNIVERSITY OF ALABAMA
AS THE OUTSTANDING COLLEGE FOOTBALL PLAYER
IN THE UNITED STATES FOR
2009

ALL MINE ## THE OWNERS OF THE PACKERS ARE ACTUALLY 360,000 INDIVIDUAL SHAREHOLDERS.

← Green Bay

`HOLDING OUT` THE FIRST PLAYER EVER DRAFTED NEVER PLAYED IN THE NFL.

University of Chicago halfback Jay Berwanger had two historic firsts: He won the first Heisman Trophy (1935), and he was the top pick of the NFL's inaugural draft. Going first didn't mean big riches for the star runner, though. The Eagles drafted him and traded him to the Bears, who couldn't meet Berwanger's salary demands. Berwanger instead became a foam-rubber salesman while also trying to become an Olympic decathlete. He never played pro football.

`TICKTOCK` THERE ARE LESS THAN 11 MINUTES OF ACTION IN AN AVERAGE FOOTBALL GAME.

Next time you watch an NFL game, take notice of how often there just isn't much going on. Along with commercial breaks and halftime, large parts of the game involve players standing in a huddle, getting organized before the ball is snapped, or waiting for an official to announce a call. According to *The Wall Street Journal*, if you took all of that inaction away, an average NFL game would last less than 11 minutes! And think about this: Average NFL telecasts devote 56% of a three-hour game to showing replays.

BROS PEYTON AND ELI MANNING ARE THE ONLY SIBLINGS TO PLAY QUARTERBACK IN THE SUPER BOWL.

The famous Manning brothers, Peyton and Eli, managed to do something father Archie never could: They quarterbacked teams to the Super Bowl. In fact, the Manning brothers each have two world titles. Eli won both with the Giants, and Peyton won one with the Colts and later the Broncos, in his final season. The Mannings also remain the only brothers to have won Super Bowl MVP Awards.

COINCIDENCE? ALL–TIME RUSHING LEADER EMMITT SMITH HAD 937 YARDS IN HIS ROOKIE SEASON, 1990, AND 937 YARDS IN HIS 15TH AND FINAL SEASON, 2004.

937 YARDS 1990

937 YARDS 2004

Over 15 NFL seasons, Emmitt Smith rushed for 18,355 yards, more than anyone in league history. And, oddly enough, he rushed for the exact same amount in his first and last seasons. As a 21-year-old rookie playing for the Cowboys in 1990, Smith rushed for 937 yards on 241 carries (a 3.9 average). And in 2004, as a 35-year-old in his second season with the Arizona Cardinals, Smith ran for 937 yards on 267 carries (a 3.5 average) to close out his career.

CLASSIC **THE BROWNS ARE THE ONLY TEAM WITH NO LOGO ON THEIR HELMETS.**

Not only are the Browns the lone team with a blank helmet, but they're also the only team named after a specific person: Paul Brown, the franchise's first head coach. (So, no, they're not named after the color.) Brown always insisted that their logo was their helmet, because nothing is more important than the team. The Browns briefly painted uniform numbers on the helmets, from 1957 through 1960, and used similar helmets as alternate uniforms from 2006 through 2008. They also created a CB logo to place on the helmet for the 1965 season, but they ultimately decided against using it.

BUMMER **THE 2008 LIONS ARE THE ONLY 0–16 TEAM IN NFL HISTORY.**

PRECIOUS METAL

THE SUPER BOWL TROPHY COSTS $50,000.

For a football player, the Lombardi Trophy costs years of hard work and sacrifice. For the NFL, which provides the trophy for the Super Bowl champion every winter, it costs . . . about $50,000. Named after Packers Hall of Fame coach Vince Lombardi, the trophy's sterling silver alone is worth approximately $3,500, and the high-end manufacturing by Tiffany & Co. to produce the unique trophy drives the price tag way up. That price tag, however, didn't stop Ravens coach Jim Harbaugh from buying every member of Baltimore's staff their very own Lombardi Trophy after the team's victory in Super Bowl XLVII!

$50,000

Let's compare, shall we?

$15,000

$13,500

$11,000

MLB COMMISSIONER'S TROPHY

You've got to play some hardball if you are going to win this trophy. The World Series winner gets this sterling silver beauty. It's 24 inches tall and weighs approximately 30 pounds. The 30 flags symbolize each team in Major League Baseball. The Commissioner's Trophy was first introduced in 1967, though it didn't get an official name until 1985. It's the only major North American league trophy that is not named after a specific person.

LARRY O'BRIEN NBA CHAMPIONSHIP TROPHY

Basketball's world champion takes home a sterling silver trophy plated in 24-karat gold. Depicting a ball going into a basket, it was originally known as the World Championship Trophy. Then it was the Walter A. Brown Trophy, named for the longtime Boston Celtics owner after his death. Since 1985, it's been named after Larry O'Brien, a former NBA commissioner. Sought after by sports' tallest athletes, the trophy is just 24 inches high and weighs approximately 14½ pounds.

NHL STANLEY CUP

The Cup was originally purchased for $48.67, with Lord Stanley of Preston planning to award it to Canada's top amateur team. Instead, it was awarded to the winner of a challenge tournament and later the NHL champion. Rather than handing out a new trophy every year, the same Stanley Cup is passed down to the NHL champion at the end of each season. Every player on the winning team is inscribed on a trophy band. When the bands are filled up, the oldest is sent to the Hall of Fame and a new one is added.

LET THE SUN SHINE UNIVERSITY OF PHOENIX STADIUM, HOME TO THE CARDINALS, ROLLS THE FIELD OUT OF THE STADIUM BETWEEN GAMES SO THE GRASS CAN GROW IN A NATURAL ENVIRONMENT.

This also allows the stadium to hold other events, like concerts, without having to worry about damaging the turf.

MUST BE THE WATER SIX OF THE 33 HALL OF FAME QBS ARE FROM THE SAME AREA IN WESTERN PENNSYLVANIA.

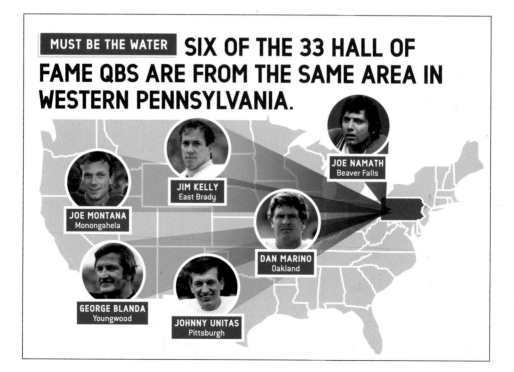

JOE NAMATH
Beaver Falls

JIM KELLY
East Brady

JOE MONTANA
Monongahela

DAN MARINO
Oakland

GEORGE BLANDA
Youngwood

JOHNNY UNITAS
Pittsburgh

SPRING CHICKEN SEAN MCVAY BECAME THE YOUNGEST HEAD COACH IN NFL HISTORY WHEN HE TOOK OVER THE L.A. RAMS AT AGE 30.

He was younger than the star left tackle the team signed soon after, 35-year-old Andrew Whitworth.

OLDIE BUT GOODIE TOM COUGHLIN IS THE OLDEST COACH TO LEAD A TEAM TO A SUPER BOWL VICTORY.

At least as of 2016. Coughlin was 65 when he led his Giants past the Patriots in February 2012 in Super Bowl XLVI. The coach he defeated, Bill Belichick, was 64 when he led the Pats to a title five years later.

REDSKINS KICKER MARK MOSELEY IS THE ONLY SPECIAL TEAMS PLAYER EVER NAMED NFL MVP.

There were a lot of oddities during the 1982 season, which was cut to nine games due to a player strike. Mark Moseley was the last of the NFL's straight-on kickers, using a square-toe kicking shoe to get added distance. He hit 20 of 21 field goal attempts, a then-record 95.2%. (That stat made up for his three missed extra points.)

TWO DEFENSIVE PLAYERS HAVE WON MVP: ALAN PAGE AND LAWRENCE TAYLOR.

Alan Page, the Vikings' tackle, became the first defensive player to win MVP when he took home the award in 1971. In more than 40 years since then, only pass-rushing superstar Lawrence Taylor of the Giants has managed to overcome the NFL's offense-first bias. LT took home the MVP award in 1986.

ALAN PAGE

LAWRENCE TAYLOR

DESMOND HOWARD IS THE ONLY SPECIAL TEAMS PLAYER TO WIN SUPER BOWL MVP.

The 1991 Heisman Trophy winner, Desmond Howard, was considered a disappointment in his NFL career. (He was the fourth pick of the 1991 draft but never developed as a receiver.) But for one night, he outshone the rest on football's biggest stage. His 32-yard punt return for the Packers set up the game's first score, and a 34-yard return in the second quarter set up a field goal. Howard sealed the game with a 99-yard kickoff return TD in the third quarter, overshadowing stars like Hall of Famers Brett Favre (246 yards, two TD passes) and Reggie White (three sacks).

CHUCK HOWLEY IS THE ONLY PLAYER FROM A LOSING TEAM TO BE NAMED SUPER BOWL MVP.

Talk about a bittersweet achievement. In Super Bowl V, the Cowboys' linebacker intercepted two passes and recovered a fumble, but it wasn't enough: The Baltimore Colts scored 10 fourth-quarter points in their 16–13 victory. Chuck Howley was the first non-QB to win Super Bowl MVP and is still the only losing player to receive the award. After the game, Howley declined to accept the award because of the loss.

COMBO PLATTER THE EAGLES AND THE STEELERS ONCE COMBINED TO MAKE A SINGLE TEAM.

In 1943, teams were struggling to fill out their rosters, as many players were fighting in World War II. The two Pennsylvania teams, the Eagles and the Steelers, decided to put their rivalry aside and join forces. For one season, the teams played together. The official record book refers to them as the Phil-Pitt Combine, but in true celebrity nickname fashion, they were better known as the Steagles.

BIG BOUNCE

THE TERM *SUPER BOWL* WAS INSPIRED BY THE TOY SUPER BALL.

Truthfully, no one is sure exactly how the biggest event in sports got its name. But the legend is that Lamar Hunt, the Chiefs' owner and AFL founder, came up with the name when he saw his kids playing with the toy bouncy ball.

SOUTHPAW

STEVE YOUNG WAS THE FIRST LEFTY QB TO MAKE THE HALL OF FAME, IN 2005.

Not bad, considering the slow start to the southpaw's pro career. Young spent two seasons playing for the Los Angeles Express of the United States Football League, then joined the Tampa Bay Bucs after the USFL folded. After two rough seasons there, he was traded to San Francisco, where he backed up Joe Montana for four seasons before becoming a star. Former Oakland Raiders QB Ken Stabler, also a lefty, was inducted into the Hall in 2016.

HANG TIGHT THE PACKERS' SEASON–TICKET WAITING LIST HAS MORE THAN 100,000 NAMES. THE TEAM SAYS THE AVERAGE WAIT FOR TICKETS IS 30 YEARS.

Every year, the Packers award season tickets to a few hundred applicants. Joining the waiting list is free, but the tickets aren't. So, for instance, in 2016, approximately 900 fans on the waiting list were offered season tickets, and 700 of those fans chose to buy them.

GRAMPS BRETT FAVRE AND JERRY RICE ARE THE ONLY NONKICKERS TO PLAY IN 300 OR MORE CAREER GAMES.

FAVRE

Even first-round picks last fewer than 10 years in the NFL on average. Playing 10 years in the league would be 160 regular-season games if a player doesn't miss a single game (a serious challenge in such a physical sport). That makes the accomplishments of Hall of Famers Brett Favre and Jerry Rice even more amazing. Favre started 297 consecutive games at one point, first for the Packers and then for the Vikings, an NFL record. (It's 321 straight starts if you include the playoffs.) Rice suffered two knee injuries in 1997, when he was in his mid-30s, but returned to play seven more full seasons. In fact, in his final NFL season, in 2004, the 42-year-old Rice tied another record: He became one of nine players to appear in 17 games since the NFL-AFL merger in 1970. He was traded from the Raiders to the Seahawks midseason. The transaction occurred after Seattle's bye week but before Oakland's, so Rice ended up playing an extra game.

RICE

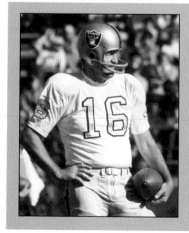

Respect Your Elders

The oldest player in NFL history was George Blanda. A quarterback and a placekicker over his career (he played during an era when few teams used specialized kickers), Blanda no longer played as a starting QB after the 1966 season, when he was 39. But he stuck around as a kicker for another nine seasons (still throwing the occasional pass). He played his final game in 1975, at 48 years and 109 days old.

BREAK! **THE HUDDLE WAS INVENTED BY PAUL HUBBARD, A DEAF QB AT GALLAUDET UNIVERSITY.**

In the 1890s, Hubbard used the huddle so he could relay signals to his deaf and hard-of-hearing teammates. It's one of the few elements from the game's early years that is still used by quarterbacks (like Cam Newton) today.

HAPPY RETURNS **DEVIN HESTER IS THE ONLY PLAYER TO BEGIN A SUPER BOWL WITH A KICKOFF RETURN FOR A TOUCHDOWN.**

Talk about starting off the game on the right foot. Bears rookie Devin Hester had six return touchdowns during the 2006 regular season, including two kickoff return scores in one game! Most teams had been opting to send kickoffs short against the Bears to avoid the speedster. To open Super Bowl XLI, however, the Colts kicked it deep, and Hester made them pay. He returned the opening kick 92 yards for a touchdown. But it wasn't enough: The Colts came back to win 29–17.

SAD FACE ONLY FOUR TEAMS HAVE NEVER PLAYED IN A SUPER BOWL.

The Lions, Browns, Texans, and Jaguars have never made it to the Big Game. In fact, poor Cleveland is the only NFL city to have never played in or hosted a Super Bowl!

BUH-BYE

NFL PLAYERS HAVE THE SHORTEST AVERAGE CAREERS.

MLB (baseball) 5.6 years
NHL (hockey) 5.5 years
NBA (basketball) 4.8 years
NFL (football) 3.3 years

WACKY WEATHER

IN A 1988 PLAYOFF GAME, THE FOG WAS SO THICK ON THE FIELD THAT OFFICIALS ANNOUNCED TO FANS WHAT HAPPENED AFTER EVERY PLAY.

The Bears had just taken a 17–6 lead on the visiting Eagles when a thick fog rolled into Soldier Field. From the second quarter on, visibility on the field was limited to 10 to 15 yards. The Bears held on for a 20–12 victory in the Fog Bowl, which one Chicago fan summed up perfectly: "Best game I've never seen!"

IT PAYS # SUPER BOWL TICKETS HAVE GOTTEN EXPENSIVE. VERY EXPENSIVE.

The priciest ticket for Super Bowl I (then known as the AFL-NFL World Championship Game) was $12. For Super Bowl 50 in 2016, the least expensive ticket available to the public via the secondary market was almost $3,000.

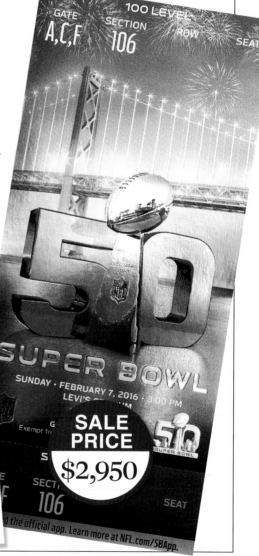

SNOOZE THE LAST SCORELESS GAME IN NFL HISTORY WAS IN 1943.

On November 7 of that year, the Lions and the Giants faced off at Detroit's Briggs Stadium on a rainy, muddy day. Both teams were shorthanded due to players leaving to fight in World War II. It also didn't help that Detroit's Augie Lio missed three field goals, including a 15-yarder.

LIONS 0   :00   GIANTS 0

BALL ON | DOWN | YDS TO GO | QTR

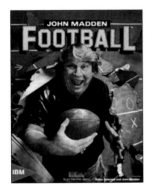

GAMER THE ORIGINAL *MADDEN* VIDEO GAME TOOK FOUR YEARS TO BUILD.

Electronic Arts founder Trip Hawkins approached John Madden, then a retired Oakland Raiders coach and a football commentator, about helping on a football simulation video game in 1984. Madden insisted he would only do it if the game featured 11-on-11 football, something never done in a video game before (mostly because computers couldn't handle the memory required). It took game producers four years to make the first version of *Madden*, released in 1988 for the Apple II series of computers. And even then, because of the 22 players moving at once, the game ran very slowly. More powerful computers and gaming consoles make current versions of *Madden* a breeze to play, and EA has sold more than 100 million copies.

PAINT JOB REFEREES STARTED WEARING STRIPED SHIRTS BECAUSE OF A GAME THAT TOOK PLACE IN 1920.

In the early days of football, referees often wore white shirts. And sometimes, when one of the teams wore white uniforms, that caused problems. During a collegiate game between Michigan State and Arizona, referee Lloyd Olds was wearing a white uniform that looked a lot like Arizona's all-white uniforms. He was mistaken for a player a few times. After that game, he had the idea that would change referee fashion forever: a black-and-white striped shirt. Now no matter what colors teams wear, the officials are never wearing the same thing.

SHADY DEAL MOST FOOTBALL STADIUMS ARE BUILT FACING NORTH AND SOUTH SO THAT THE SUN NEVER INTERFERES WITH A PLAY.

Otherwise, for an afternoon game, a sun setting in the West could blind one team as it heads upfield and force the other team's receivers to stare into the sun when they look back for a pass.

YOU GOTTA EAT SUPER BOWL GAME DAY RANKS SECOND IN AMOUNT OF FOOD CONSUMED.

When it comes to the day during which people in the U.S. eat the most food, Thanksgiving ranks first. Super Bowl Sunday, an unofficial holiday, ranks second. These are some of the most popular foods at Super Bowl parties and how much America eats of each.

15 MILLION PIZZA PIES
(according to *Pizza Today*)

11.2 MILLION POUNDS OF CHIPS
(according to the National Restaurant Association)

278 MILLION AVOCADOS
(according to the Hass Avocado Board)

1.3 BILLION CHICKEN WINGS
(according to the National Chicken Council)

SKILLS TO MASTER

Being a fan is about more than just knowing everything about football. It's about doing things the right way too.

GET AN AUTOGRAPH

Getting your favorite player's John Hancock isn't always easy, but here are some tips to improve your chances.

1 Know faces Players don't always wear their uniforms, and since they're usually wearing helmets when they're on TV, a lot of people don't recognize them in person. Being able to (politely) call out who's who can be the difference between getting a signature and being ignored.

2 Go camping Getting an autograph at an actual game is tough; arrive as early as possible, and try to find where players enter and exit the stadium. More players will sign at training camp practices, many of which are open to fans.

3 Mail it in Can't make it to a game or practice? Try mailing a football card or photo to get signed. Send it to the team's address, and be sure to include a handwritten note and a self-addressed, stamped envelope.

MAKE AN
OVER-THE-SHOULDER CATCH

The toughest catch in football is when you're running straight downfield, looking back over your shoulder. Receiver Larry Fitzgerald explains how to make it look easy.

1 When looking back, focus on the nose of the ball. That will give you the best idea of where it's coming down.

2 Catch the front of the ball, hauling it in with the pads of your fingers, not your palms.

3 When you get a step on the defender, be sure to position your body between him and where the ball is coming down.

4 Once you've made the catch, tuck the ball into your body, carrying it with the arm closer to the sideline.

THROW A SPIRAL

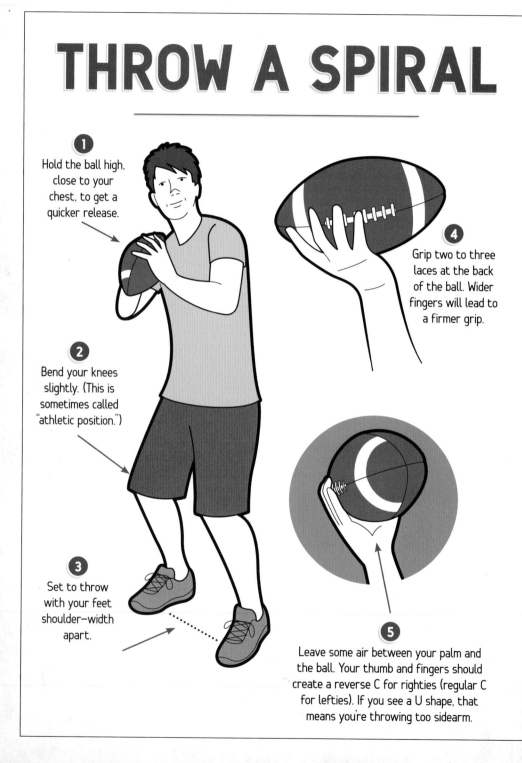

1 Hold the ball high, close to your chest, to get a quicker release.

2 Bend your knees slightly. (This is sometimes called "athletic position.")

3 Set to throw with your feet shoulder–width apart.

4 Grip two to three laces at the back of the ball. Wider fingers will lead to a firmer grip.

5 Leave some air between your palm and the ball. Your thumb and fingers should create a reverse C for righties (regular C for lefties). If you see a U shape, that means you're throwing too sidearm.

8 Your left shoulder should pull down and away when you throw, allowing for an over-the-top motion.

6 Rotate your hips and open your left shoulder toward the target.

9 Your forearm and biceps should form an L shape. The closer your biceps is to your ear, the more over-the-top (and better) your throw.

11 Flick your wrist slightly as you release. Your index finger should be the last finger to come off the ball.

7 Step toward your target. The step should be about six inches; overstriding will affect your mechanics.

10 Transfer your weight to your front foot as you throw.

12 At the end of your release, your thumb should be pointed at your opposite hip.

13 Be proud of your super spiral!

FOLD A PAPER FOOTBALL

Nothing passes the time like some good ol' tabletop football.
Here's how to make a paper football the right way.

1 Fold an 8½-by-11 piece of paper in half long ways.

2 Fold each side in half again, toward the center.

3 Now fold one more time toward the center.

4 Starting at the top, fold into triangles (along dotted lines).

5 Keep folding until you run out of paper.

6 Fold the last triangle over to create a tab.

7 Tuck the excess paper tab into the pocket of the triangle.

8 Find some space on your kitchen table, grab a friend, and have him set up goalposts with his fingers (index fingers touching, thumbs pointing up). Here's the kick!

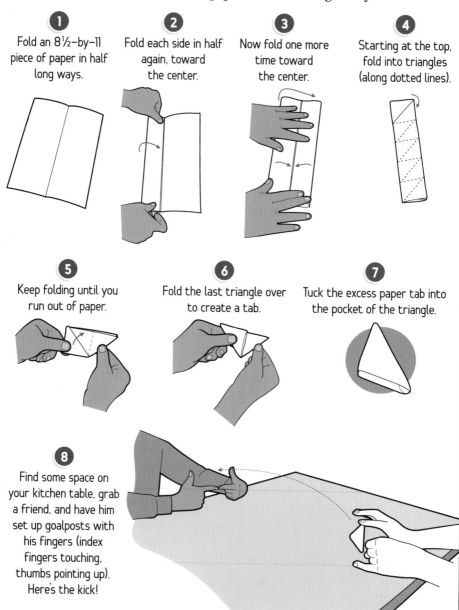

LOSE WITH DIGNITY

It's the harsh but simple truth: Only once in the Super Bowl era has a team won every game over the course of a season. At some point, your favorite team is going to take an L. Here's how to deal with it.

1 **Don't second-guess ("If only that one play. . . .")** The tipped pass that turned into an interception. The field goal that *doinked* off the upright. The controversial penalty in the fourth quarter. Every game is full of good and bad breaks, and fans tend to remember the bad ones. Chances are, your team also had a couple of lucky bounces along the way too.

2 **Congratulate the other guy** That other team fought just as hard as yours did. And while you might not like the players, you can respect them. If you have a friend who was rooting for the opposing team, give him or her a handshake and a pat on the back.

3 **Focus on the positives** There are 53 players on a roster, and it's doubtful that every single one of them played poorly. Focus on who played well, especially young players and rookies. There's always the next game!

CELEBRATE A TOUCHDOWN

It's the biggest play of a game. Here's how to celebrate when your team puts six points on the board.

① **Never have food in your lap when your team is in the red zone** It's all fun and games until the nachos go *splat* on a white rug. Enjoy a snack, but when your team is within striking distance and excitement is about to get the best of you, make sure the food is safely out of reach on a nearby table.

② **Unleash your signature celebration** From the Lambeau Leap to the Gronk Spike, everyone should have a go-to celebration. As a fan, you should have one too. Come up with some original moves to celebrate a TD. Leaps, spins, fist-pumps—whatever feels good to you.

③ **Congratulate your fanmates** Nothing's better than celebrating with a fellow enthusiast. If you have an elaborate celebratory handshake, go for it. And if not, use a simple high five. Not so hard that it hurts, but you want that smack!

MAKE THE ULTIMATE GAME-DAY SNACK

Two ingredients and your chips of choice. Queso is simple to make—but have a parent around, just in case.

1 **Cut processed cheese into chunks and place in a microwave-safe bowl with the diced tomatoes and green chilies** Don't even think about using fancy cheese. It won't melt properly.

2 **Microwave on high for five minutes** For easy cooking and easier cleanup, use a microwave (instead of a double boiler or crock pot). Just be sure to cover the bowl with a napkin in case the queso bubbles. Stir after three minutes and then continue cooking. Don't forget to use oven mitts! Your queso will be hot!

3 **Enjoy your liquid gold** Stir, and share with friends and family . . . just be sure to keep some for yourself!

UNLEASH A PERFECT PUNT

The best punters will tell you: It's all about the drop. Catch the snap, and grip with the pads of your fingers. Hold the ball laces up, and drop the pigskin with as little spin as possible.

Take two steps forward. Catch the ball and step with your kicking foot, then your plant foot. Your momentum brings you forward as you kick, especially as you follow through.

As you swing your kicking leg forward, your toe should be pointed straight ahead. Make contact with the ball using the top of your foot.

DRESS APPROPRIATELY WHEN YOU'RE GOING TO A GAME

Think your attire can't help or hurt your team? You're right, it probably can't. But that doesn't mean you can't have your own uniform to look good and feel lucky on game day.

Coat You can always take it off and put it on your seat, but remember: Cold days always seem colder when you're staying in one spot.

Long-sleeved T Especially crucial for autumn in cold-weather stadiums. It keeps you warm and allows you to slip a jersey on over it.

Jersey Of your favorite player. Bonus points if it's not the QB. (More bonus points if it's a throwback jersey.)

Hat Baseball cap to shield the sun on a hot day, wool cap if it's cold.

Pitch pipe Make sure you're in the right key for your team's fight song.

Football For throwing around in the parking lot. (You probably can't bring it into the stadium.)

Sharpies A must if you're chasing autographs. (Get there early!)

Foam finger A classic. And it doubles as a hand-warmer.

Lucky socks If your team's on a winning streak, don't wash 'em! (Just don't tell your parents.)

Clean underwear You didn't forget, did you?

PRACTICE ON YOUR OWN

Got some downtime this weekend? It's easy to hone your skills in the backyard or at the park.

① Use cups as cones Don't have traditional cones? Set up eight to 10 plastic cups (maybe weight each one with a rock), and get going on some agility and speed drills. Because one thing every great player at every position has in common: good footwork.

② Throw the ball in the garbage Literally. Just make sure it's empty. Many NFL quarterbacks train this way to develop touch on deep throws (aka "dropping it in the bucket"). A recycling bin or laundry basket works too.

③ Get over the pile O.K., this one is mostly for fun. Nothing simulates a goal-line stand better than a pile of leaves in the fall. Get two arms on the ball and a running start, then launch yourself deep into the pile for a touchdown.

KEEP THE FAITH

It's a fact of life for NFL fans: Your team is going to go through some rough years. Here's how to stay positive.

1 Baby steps Keep your expectations in check. If your guys went 1–15, they're probably not winning the Super Bowl the next year. But maybe they have a chance to go 7–9. And maybe they have a chance to win a game against a hated rival. And then maybe the year after that, they have a chance to get to the playoffs. And then maybe the following year. . . .

2 Youth gone wild If your team's present isn't so bright, you have to look to the future. And that means identifying the rising stars on the roster. Those are the guys who will help turn your team into a winner.

3 Today's doormat, tomorrow's dynasty A decade before Tom Brady led the Patriots to their first Super Bowl title, New England won a total of nine games over a three-year span. Who would've thought that a sixth-round draft pick could turn a last-place team into a modern dynasty? Things can change quickly and unexpectedly.

DRAFT A FANTASY FOOTBALL TEAM

If you can't be general manager of an NFL team, do the next best thing and run a fantasy football team.

2 Get studying There are plenty of magazines that come out every summer that will give you the basic knowledge of who to target and who to avoid in drafts. Combine that with some Internet updates (injuries, benchings, etc.), and you should be ready to go.

1 Find a league The best leagues are ones between friends. But if none of your buddies are into football, have your parents help you pick an online league.

3 Understand strategy Oddly enough, quarterbacks are not particularly valuable in fantasy. The best teams are usually built around a strong group of running backs and receivers, with QBs becoming complementary players.

4 **Draft time = party time** Fantasy football draft day is an unofficial holiday. As long as you prepared, you should be plenty relaxed as the actual draft unfolds. Drafting online is fine, but it's much better to get your friends together, get a couple of pizzas, and enjoy the camaraderie.

5 **The draft is only Step 1** The season doesn't end with the draft. Every NFL season, a handful of surprise stars emerge. Get ready to shake up your roster to keep improving.

6 **Not just Sundays** Remember: Most weeks, there's a game on Thursday! It's a lesson many fantasy owners learn the hard way. Be sure to check your lineup on Thursday afternoons as well as Sunday and Monday mornings.

WATCH YOUR FAVORITE TEAM'S GAME

Because, as a fan, nothing is more important than game day.

1 **Rally friends and family**
If you have to go it alone, that's O.K. But games are always better when you're surrounded by fellow fans.

2 **Prepare a feast**
Or at least some chips and queso (*page 79*). You can't root on an empty stomach.

3 **Turn off your phone!** One last check before kickoff, then the game should have your undivided attention. (Maybe one quick check at halftime.)

4 **Be smart about bathroom breaks**
Hold it until halftime if you're able. But if you can't, the best time is right after a touchdown. (If you're going to miss any action, make it an extra point or a kickoff.)

5 **Put away the remote** You think you're just going to check on the other game and flip back quickly, and the next thing you know, you just missed your team's 91-yard TD. If your favorite team is playing, it stays on the TV.

APPRECIATE GREATNESS

1 **Listen to the announcers** Here's a hint: If it's a truly great play, the announcers won't scream nonstop. They'll give their excited take quickly, then let the crowd noise take over, because they need a few moments to digest what happened.

2 **Dive deep** Understand the athleticism that goes into great plays. The incredible focus it takes to make a diving catch. The exceptional balance of a rusher bouncing off tackles as he stays on his feet. The toughness of a quarterback to stand in and deliver the perfect pass as a blitzer crunches his midsection.

3 **It's in the details** There are always a couple of things to pick up on when you watch the replays. For instance, on Odell Beckham Jr.'s stupendous catch *(above)*, did you notice that it wasn't just a one-handed catch—it was a three-fingered catch?! How did the Giants celebrate? How did the Cowboys and the officials react? There's plenty to see on every play, and especially on the great ones.

THINK LIKE A COACH

The ultimate football fans also know how to talk X's and O's. Consider this a crash course in NFL Coaching 101.

OFFENSIVE STRATEGIES

1. RUNNING GAME

The running game seems simple enough: Big guys block anything that moves, and the runner follows behind them. But, like many things in the NFL, everything is more complicated than it looks on TV. Run-blocking takes an incredible amount of chemistry and teamwork among blockers, which is why the best offensive lines are often the ones that have played together for a while. The goal is to block players on the defense's first level (defensive linemen) and second level (linebackers). Many times one blocker will start on a defensive lineman, then "pass him off" to a teammate and go block a linebacker. To be able to know exactly when your teammate is about to pass off a defender to you, or the exact moment the guy next to you is ready to take over your block, takes as much chemistry as any connection on the football field.

Sweet! Thanks for the opening, guys.

Man Blocking

There's a reason man blocking (sometimes called "power blocking") has been around forever: It works. And it's simple. Or at least the idea is simple. Before the play, the blockers (offensive linemen and any tight ends or backs) identify their assignments, or whom they're going to block. The running back has an assigned hole that he is supposed to run through, under the assumption that his linemen open that hole. Typical man-blocking schemes often involve pulling linemen. That's when a blocker loops around to another part of the formation—like the left guard looping around to the right side—to create some deception on a play. This is often the system for teams with massive offensive linemen who are good at overpowering opponents in close quarters.

Outside Zone Blocking

This is a relatively modern form of run blocking that was developed in the late 1980s. But it really came into fashion with the Broncos' great running offenses of the 1990s. Zone blocking involves the entire offensive line, as a unit, moving to one side or the other at the snap and essentially resetting the play to the left or right. As the line moves, each blocker then identifies a defender in his zone that he's going to block. The running back follows those blockers and identifies a hole to run through as the play develops. Then the back makes a hard cut upfield and tries to find daylight. To run a zone-heavy blocking scheme, you need more nimble (and often smaller) offensive linemen up front.

OFFENSIVE STRATEGIES

2. PROTECT THE PASSER

The modern NFL is a pass-happy game, and nothing is more important to an offense than good quarterback play. And good quarterback play never happens if the QB keeps getting hit or knocked down. A chess match often plays out between the offensive line and the pass rushers, especially when it comes to individual battles on the end. Pass rushers have moves—and offensive linemen do too. Some teams teach a half-dozen different "sets," ways for blockers to deal with oncoming rushers. There are three basic sets. With a vertical set, the lineman moves straight back before getting ready to block. In an angle set, the blocker moves back at an angle, rather than straight back. And there's a quick set, in which the blocker moves forward and attacks the pass rusher, often on a quick passing play. On a quick pass, a blocker can also use a cut block to take out a defender's legs and prevent him from jumping up and swatting the ball. Here are some of the overall strategies offenses use to get the passing game going.

Extra Help

While the offensive line is mostly responsible for building a pocket to protect the quarterback, other players help too. Sometimes tight ends will "stay in" to help double team a dangerous edge pass rusher or even be asked to block a pass rusher themselves. And pass protection is now a crucial skill for running backs. They are often asked to "pick up"

blitzers, or to get in the way of those unexpected pass rushers that the offensive linemen can't account for. Running backs and tight ends can also use "chip blocks" (such as the one you see above, executed by a tight end). They'll go out for a pass but on the way land a little block on a pass rusher, attempting to knock that defender off track.

Get a Move On, or Get Rid of It!

Of course, the quarterback himself can keep from getting sacked. Many teams will have the QB roll out—or even sprint out—to the right or the left by design. Pass rushers planning on attacking a spot behind the center then have to change their plans after the snap. The downside for the offense is that it cuts the field in half; the QB can really only throw to the side he's moving toward. But the easiest way for a QB to avoid a sack? Get rid of the ball quickly. Maestros like Peyton Manning and Tom Brady have thrived at reading defenses before the snap. This can be done by having a receiver go in motion. Whether or not a defender follows the receiver can tip off whether the D is playing man or zone coverage. Or sometimes a hard count (a fake snap call) leads to the D giving away who's blitzing. And if the QB has a good idea of what the defense is doing, he has gained a big advantage and can get rid of the ball soon after the snap.

OFFENSIVE STRATEGIES

3. THROUGH THE AIR

"**R**un 10 steps, turn around, and I'll throw you the ball." That's what the passing game is in the backyard, but things are a little more complicated in the pros. In most NFL offenses, both the quarterback and his pass catchers have to read the defense. In fact, in many offenses, the quarterback's "progressions" (the order in which he'll look at his receivers) will depend on what coverage the defense is playing. Many teams also use "option routes"—a receiver's route will depend on what kind of coverage the defense is playing. No matter the offense, almost every passing game involves a "checkdown" option, a receiver who runs a shorter route and is the last option if everyone else is covered. It all leads to a complicated system in which the quarterback must have great chemistry with his pass catchers since both the QB and his receivers must make the same read. Ultimately many of the miscues you see over the course of a game (interceptions and incomplete passes) are the fault of the receiver as much as they are the fault of the quarterback.

You throw it, and I'll be there.

West Coast And Air Coryell

The modern passing game has become a mashup of different styles. There's the West Coast offense, which typically relies on shorter, high-percentage passes. These offenses lean heavily on running backs and on tight ends acting as receivers, and usually spread the defense across the field horizontally. In typical West Coast systems, timing is of the utmost importance. There's also the Air Coryell system, named after longtime Chargers coach Don Coryell. This is a system that sends multiple receivers on deep routes, stretching the defense horizontally and vertically.

Getting Open

Offenses use varying philosophies when it comes to route running. Some use "isolation" routes. That means a coach is telling a receiver, "That guy covering you? Shake him and get open." And some teams use combinations or other tricks to get their pass catchers open. "Rub routes" (think of a pick in basketball) are a way to get a receiver away from a pesky cover man. Receivers will cross, with one of them trying to "accidentally" run into the defender guarding his teammate. Teams will also line up receivers close to each other in "bunch" and "stack" formations to try to (1) confuse the defense and (2) keep certain receivers from getting pressed by a defensive back at the line of scrimmage.

DEFENSIVE STRATEGIES

1. GET THE QB

A sk any defensive coach in the NFL about the best way to stop a high-powered passing game, and they'll all tell you the same thing: Pressure the quarterback. It's not all about sacks. Hits just after a pass and general pressure can throw a quarterback off his game. And pressure on the QB leads to more turnovers—the NFL's biggest game-changers—than anything else. Of course, saying you want to get to the quarterback is one thing. Actually succeeding is another. Every coach in the NFL would love to have someone like J.J. Watt, Von Miller, or Khalil Mack on his team, a guy who can just line up and get to the quarterback. But for teams that aren't so lucky, there are still plenty of ways to create pressure on opposing QBs.

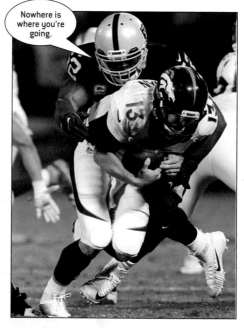

Nowhere is where you're going.

Blitz!

It's the most common way to get more pressure. Rather than just sending the first line of the pass rush—the defensive line—a coach sends an extra pass rusher or two, with linebackers and/or defensive backs charging at the QB. The goal is to catch offenses by surprise, either because they didn't realize the blitzing player was coming or because there were too many players to block. Of course, the more players who blitz, the fewer players who are left in coverage. Leaving multiple receivers in one-on-one coverage is always a huge risk. Some teams will use zone coverage behind a blitz. (This is a strategy of the modern Steelers.) Most will have their defensive backs guard against shorter routes, anticipating that the quarterback will have to throw the ball quickly. Teams will also sometimes fake blitzes, putting a player close to the line of scrimmage but then dropping him into coverage to stress the QB.

Twists and Stunts

Maybe a defense doesn't have a top pass rusher but isn't too keen on blitzing, either. One solution might be twists and stunts. A stunt is a combination play typically run by two defensive linemen. One player will push forward into the blockers, while his teammate loops around him and, hopefully, the blockers as well. The thought is that the move will create confusion among the blockers, and they'll react late (or sometimes not at all) to the second rusher. A recent trend has been to create even more pressure up the middle, enough to block the quarterback's line of vision. That can be done by blitzing inside linebackers or just having exceptional players at defensive tackle.

DEFENSIVE STRATEGIES

2. STOPPING THE RUN

I t's an old adage that still holds some truth today: The best defenses are the ones that can stuff the run. And really, there's nothing more degrading for defensive guys than letting a bunch of offensive players push them around. So how to go about stopping the run? Different teams have different philosophies. Many have their biggest linemen (those massive tackles sometimes referred to as "run stuffers") act as blockers themselves. Their job is to keep offensive linemen from getting to the "second level," where the linebackers are. Then those linebackers can run free; they're responsible for stepping up and making the tackle on the ballcarrier. As for the linebackers, the best ones can anticipate plays based on how the blockers move, not just by looking for the ballcarrier. The rest is a matter of making the tackle.

The play's going that way.

Mind Your Gaps and Set The Edge

Stopping the run is about being physical. And it's also about being disciplined. At the start of a play, defensive players are responsible for "gaps," the holes in the line through which a running play might go. If a player abandons his gap, that's when you see big runs happen. Perhaps just as important as plugging any gap is taking care of "the edge." The player responsible for "setting the edge" has one job: Make sure the ballcarrier doesn't run around the outside of the defense; if he does that, he's going to have a lot of open space in front of him. Many times, a defensive end or outside linebacker is responsible for setting the edge. But some teams will use cornerbacks who tackle well to step in and do the job.

Stack the Box

Imagine you are looking down at the field from overhead (like a defensive coordinator might). Draw a rectangle around the defensive linemen and the linebackers; that is "the box." Typically, the more defenders a team puts in the box, the better chance it has at stopping a run play. When you hear the term *stacking the box*, that usually means there is a defensive back joining the linebackers near the line of scrimmage. A seven-man box (made up of linemen and linebackers) is a basic alignment. An eight-man box? That means a defense is expecting the run; you will usually see that approach on first and second down.

DEFENSIVE STRATEGIES

3. COVERAGE

The secondary is, literally, the last line of defense. And in today's NFL, it's more important than ever. When it comes to stopping a passing play, the role of the defensive backfield is pretty clear: Cover the pass catchers, and if the ball comes your way, make sure it isn't caught. (And, if you can, intercept it yourself!) But few positions in football have a wider array of strategies and styles. At the most basic level: You can play man-to-man; you can play zone; or you can play a mixture of the two. For years, man defense has been the choice for units with superior talent. The job of the cornerbacks and, sometimes, safeties and linebackers, is to track a man wherever he goes (often with a safety to help on deep routes). Zone coverage involves a little more communication, with defenders "passing off" receivers to each other, depending on whose zone they are entering. For instance, a cornerback might be responsible for short routes on one side of the field. If a receiver is in his area but then runs downfield, the cornerback might have to "pass him off" to a safety behind him and then find another receiver to cover.

I got it and you didn't! Ha-ha!

Press or Play Off

The question for cornerbacks: Line up right on top of the men they cover, or back off? There are advantages to both. In press coverage, the cornerback starts right in the receiver's face and tries to "jam" him at the beginning of the play (defenders can contact receivers for the first five yards), then turn and cover him. The goal is to not only slow down that receiver but also to throw off the timing of the play. Of course, if the receiver beats the cornerback's jam, the cornerback is in trouble. Corners also play "off" the receiver, in man or zone coverage. Sometimes it's because they're facing a speedy receiver and don't want to give up the deep pass. But one big

advantage to playing off the receiver is that the cornerback can also see the quarterback, giving the corner a better chance at making an interception.

Play It Safety

Safeties are some of the most versatile players on a football field. Along with being expected to help on run plays, they are sometimes asked to cover tight ends, running backs, and receivers in man-to-man. A safety's role in pass defense often defines what coverage a team is playing. For instance, Cover 2 means that two safeties are playing back as the last line of defense. The field is cut in half, and each safety is responsible for the deep part of one half of the field. Cover 3 is sometimes also called "single high." That means one safety (normally

there are two on the field) patrols the deep middle of the field, while the other plays closer to the line of scrimmage. Cornerbacks alongside him are responsible for preventing deep plays on the outside. Teams that use zone coverage behind blitzes often have their safeties rotate into shorter zones, covering areas that the blitzing players would have normally covered.

ALL ABOUT QBS

The quarterback is the most important player of all, and NFL teams use the QB in very similar ways. Why is that? And just what does a QB do to make the offense run smoothly?

In college football, quarterbacks often pile up big rushing numbers. Why isn't that the case in the NFL?

Indeed, you might have noticed that some of the greatest quarterbacks in college football history have failed to find success in the NFL. And a lot of those quarterbacks were "running QBs." There are a few reasons quarterbacks don't have a lot of success as runners in the NFL. First, the rules are a bit different in college football. Offensive linemen are permitted to move farther downfield than in the pros, allowing teams to disguise plays that can be a run or a pass (these are called RPOs: Run/Pass Options). But mostly, NFL defenders are bigger, stronger, and definitely faster, though the field isn't any larger. That means running QBs have a tougher time getting away from NFL defenders. And when those QBs do get caught, the hits are bigger, putting them at risk of injury. (An exception is Cam Newton, who at 245 pounds is able to withstand more contact.) A QB's legs are most valuable when it comes to avoiding the pass rush. The best ones extend the play, avoiding sacks and making the defense cover receivers for longer. (Think Aaron Rodgers and Russell Wilson.) When defenders are gassed, these mobile QBs can find an open receiver downfield.

Sigh. I miss college.

So many NFL coaches use the term *win from the pocket*. That means hanging in and sticking with the passing option rather than taking off and running. The most complex passing games are designed to go through different "progressions" (the order in which the QB will look at his receivers) based on what the defense does. And the best offenses have quarterbacks who have full command of those systems.

What's with all that gesturing and yelling quarterbacks do at the line of scrimmage?

The fact is, a quarterback's job goes well beyond simply dropping back and throwing. The best ones are essentially coaches on the field. At the most basic level, the quarterback has to make sure his teammates know where to line up and what their assignments are.

• Have you ever noticed a QB pointing at a defensive player and proclaiming that he is "the Mike"? The Mike is a nickname for a middle linebacker. But this doesn't necessarily have to be a middle linebacker, just any player lined up in the middle of the defense. This is part of setting up pass protection. Maybe the left guard is responsible for blocking the first blitzer to the left of the Mike. And maybe the running back is responsible for blocking the pass rusher two players over from the Mike. Saying who the Mike is simply gets the offensive players on the same page as far as their assignments go.

• Veteran QBs can also call "audibles," changing plays at the line. Say a running play is called, but the defense has eight players near the line of scrimmage. The quarterback can check to a passing play. Or sometimes the QB simply tweaks a play. Maybe a running play was supposed to go to the left, but the defense is stacked up on that side. The QB might signal for the same play to be run to the right. QBs also can signal to individual receivers to change their routes, based on what the defense is showing before the snap.

Why go no-huddle?

The huddle is, by far, the easiest way for a quarterback to communicate the play to his teammates. So why ever go without it? One reason is simply to move the ball down the field faster (especially when playing from behind). But no-huddle creates two significant advantages. First, it prevents the defense from substituting players, and it

forces them to communicate with each other across the field. And for many veteran QBs, it gives them a chance to see how the defense is lined up and make more changes at the line. If you huddle, the quarterback might only have 10 to 15 seconds to look at the D and make changes. You might see a veteran QB like Tom Brady or Philip Rivers go no-huddle and spend 25 to 30 seconds looking at the defense and making changes to the play.

HE REMINDS ME OF...

Ever wonder just what
it was like to watch some
old-time greats on the gridiron?
To get an idea, take a look at the
modern-day players who match
these Hall of Famers' styles.

The CURRENT GUY

AARON RODGERS
Quarterback

HEIGHT, WEIGHT
6' 2", 225 pounds

TEAM
Packers

CAREER STATS
YDS: 36,827 TD: 297 INT: 72
(12 seasons)

AWARDS AND HONORS
Two-time NFL MVP
(2011, 2014),
Super Bowl XLV MVP,
five-time Pro Bowler

D uring a rough spot in 2014, Rodgers famously delivered this message to panicked Packers fans: "R-E-L-A-X." Then he led the shorthanded Packers to the second round of the playoffs. Montana was known as Joe Cool because he couldn't be rattled, even on the biggest stage. But both these quarterbacks had more than a calm demeanor. Montana was considered an undersized and generally underwhelming prospect coming out of Notre Dame in 1979. In fact, he lasted until the third round of the draft. Rodgers, too, suffered a draft-day

JOE MONTANA
Quarterback

HEIGHT, WEIGHT
6' 2", 200 pounds

TEAMS
49ers, Chiefs

CAREER STATS
YDS: 40,551 **TD:** 273
INT: 139 (15 seasons)

AWARDS AND HONORS
Two-time NFL MVP
(1989, 1990), three-time
Super Bowl MVP,
eight-time Pro Bowler

fall in 2005. Considered a potential first pick out of Cal, he lasted until the 24th pick. They both proved to be masters of versions of the West Coast offense. Both quarterbacks were adept on the move, with the ability to run for positive yardage and to escape the rush and make strong, accurate throws while in motion. Rodgers is known for getting out of trouble and then delivering the big play. Montana was too. His most famous play was nicknamed the Catch, but receiver Dwight Clark never would have hauled in that touchdown if Montana hadn't rolled to the right and, with defenders in his face, made the tough throw.

DAVID JOHNSON

Running Back

HEIGHT, WEIGHT
6' 1", 224 pounds

TEAM
Cardinals

CAREER STATS
YDS: 1,820 **TD:** 24
AVG: 4.4 (two seasons)

AWARDS AND HONORS
2016 first-team All-Pro,
2016 Pro Bowl

C oming into the NFL out of the University of Northern Iowa in 2015, no one was sure what to make of Johnson. He was a small-school prospect who was third on the Cardinals' depth chart as a rookie. But when he finally got his chance, Johnson proved to be one of the most dangerous, powerful, and versatile running backs in the league. He used his size to run over and through defenders. And he also showed skills often associated with small backs: He was able to get open and make big plays as a pass-catcher. He's considered a better pass-catcher than many wide receivers! Like Johnson, Payton came to the NFL from a

WALTER PAYTON

Running Back

HEIGHT, WEIGHT
5' 10", 200 pounds

TEAM
Bears

CAREER STATS
YDS: 16,726 **TD**: 110
AVG: 4.4 (13 seasons)

AWARDS AND HONORS
1977 NFL MVP, nine-time Pro Bowler, NFL All-Decade Team (1970s, 1980s)

small school, Jackson State. (In fact, the Walter Payton Award is given to the best offensive player in the Football Championship Subdivision, the smaller schools in Division I college football.) And, like Johnson, Payton was a big back who could punish would-be tacklers. But he earned the nickname Sweetness because of his smooth running style and ability to escape defenders like a smaller runner. He was impressive as a pass-catcher, making the grab and then gliding like a gazelle in the open field. His blend of grace and power made him the heart of a Bears team known more for its stifling defense.

The CURRENT GUY

J.J. WATT
Defensive End

HEIGHT, WEIGHT
6' 5", 290 pounds

TEAM
Texans

CAREER STATS
SACKS: 76 (six seasons)

AWARDS AND HONORS
Three-time NFL Defensive
Player of the Year (2012,
2014, 2015), four-time
first-team All-Pro, two-time
NFL sacks leader
(2012, 2015)

Watt spends a lot of time rushing the passer from the interior of the defensive line, something that White did often. And, like White, Watt's rare combination of size and athleticism makes him a nightmare for opposing blockers. White was known as the Minister of Defense. It was in part because he was devoutly religious and had become an ordained Baptist minister during his time at the University of Tennessee. But it was also because he was the most unstoppable defensive player of his era. White was not only massive, but he was also exceptionally quick and

REGGIE WHITE

Defensive End

HEIGHT, WEIGHT
6' 5", 300 pounds

TEAMS
Eagles, Packers, Panthers

CAREER STATS
SACKS: 198 (15 seasons)

AWARDS AND HONORS
Two-time NFL Defensive Player
of the Year (1987, 1998),
eight-time first-team All-Pro,
two-time NFL sacks
leader (1987, 1988)

powerful. He moved like a much smaller player but had the brute strength to toss offensive linemen aside. He became famous for a pass rush technique that combined his speed and strength, known as the hump. Lining up at defensive end, White would explode upfield as if he were trying to get around the corner. And when the offensive lineman would slide back to get into position, White would simply swat him out of the way with one hand, then move back inside for the sack. This move made him virtually unstoppable. Watt is regularly double-teamed but has the strength to just toss blockers aside. And, as was the case with White, he's at his most dangerous attacking inside, instead of trying to run around the outside edge.

The CURRENT GUY

PATRICK PETERSON
Cornerback

HEIGHT, WEIGHT
6' 1", 203 pounds

TEAM
Cardinals

CAREER STATS
INT: 20
FUMBLES RECOVERED: 10 (six seasons)

AWARDS AND HONORS
Six-time Pro Bowler,
three-time first-team All-Pro

P eterson, who has grown into a true shutdown corner, is the closest player to Sanders in today's game. They are the same height, though Peterson is built a little bit thicker. (He has slimmed down since entering the league.) Like Sanders, speed is Peterson's calling card, and he's as dangerous as Sanders was when he gets the ball in his hands. Peterson returned a league-leading four punts for TDs as a rookie in 2011. Sanders returned nine interceptions for scores in his career and another six punts and three kickoffs. His return touchdowns are second most in NFL history. Known as Prime Time and Neon Deion, Sanders was one of the biggest personalities ever to take the field. The cover corner was famous for his unique style, confidence, and

DEION SANDERS
Cornerback

HEIGHT, WEIGHT
6' 1", 190 pounds

TEAMS
Falcons, 49ers, Cowboys,
Redskins, Ravens

CAREER STATS
INT: 53
FUMBLES RECOVERED: 13 (14 seasons)

AWARDS AND HONORS
1994 NFL Defensive Player of the Year, eight-time
Pro Bowler, six-time first-team All-Pro,
NFL 1990s All-Decade Team

brash personality. His trademark "do-rag"
and flashy end zone dances were imitated
throughout the league. But as a player,
Sanders's blazing speed is what set him
apart. He could afford to play
aggressively, knowing he had the
wheels to catch up if a receiver got
behind him. There was nothing
Sanders liked more than picking off
passes and taking them back for
touchdowns. Of course, as the years
went on, it became tougher for
Sanders to get those touchdowns.
Opposing quarterbacks simply
didn't want to throw in
his direction.

The
CURRENT
GUY

VON MILLER
Outside Linebacker

HEIGHT, WEIGHT
6' 3", 250 pounds

TEAM
Broncos

CAREER STATS
SACKS: 73½ (six seasons)

AWARDS AND HONORS
Five-time Pro Bowler, three-time
first-team All-Pro, Super Bowl 50 MVP,
2011 NFL Defensive
Rookie of the Year

F or edge rushers, those sack masters who attack the quarterback from the edge of the defensive line, speed is the name of the game. And two of the fastest players to ever play the position are Miller and the fearless Jones. The two superstars, however, have used their speed in different ways. Miller is a master at using his hands to swat away the mitts of anyone trying to

DEACON JONES

Defensive End

The
OLD GUY

HEIGHT, WEIGHT
6' 5", 272 pounds

TEAMS
Rams, Chargers, Redskins

CAREER STATS
SACKS: 173½; approximation since sacks were not yet an official stat (14 seasons)

AWARDS AND HONORS
Two-time NFL Defensive Player of the Year (1967, 1968), eight-time Pro Bowler

block him. But his strengths are his flexibility and balance; he can stay at top speed while turning, allowing him to dip and fly by would-be blockers. Jones was famous for his head-slap move. It's no longer legal in the NFL (because of injury concerns), but Jones would wallop the helmet of the player trying to block him, often so hard that it would momentarily stun the opponent. He'd then have a free run at the quarterback, and no one could close on a QB faster. And in today's game? No one gets there faster than Miller.

ADRIAN PETERSON

Running Back

HEIGHT, WEIGHT
6' 1", 220 pounds

TEAM
Vikings

CAREER STATS
YDS: 11,747 TD: 97
AVG: 4.9 (nine seasons)

AWARDS AND HONORS
2012 NFL MVP, three-time
rushing champion,
seven-time Pro Bowler,
four-time first-team All-Pro

P eterson has always been considered a throwback player. The current NFL is all about passing, but the Vikings have spent the past decade relying on Peterson's playmaking abilities on the ground to keep them in games. That's because he is the rare runner with the ability to create big gains single-handedly. He has the size of a linebacker, with the explosive strength to shed defenders with ease. And once he's past the first wave of defenders, he has the track-star speed to

JIM BROWN
Running Back

HEIGHT, WEIGHT
6' 2", 232 pounds

TEAM
Browns

CAREER STATS
YDS: 12,312 **TD**: 106
AVG: 5.2 (nine seasons)

AWARDS AND HONORS
Four-time NFL MVP (1957, 1958, 1963, 1965), eight-time rushing champion, nine-time Pro Bowler, eight-time first-team All-Pro

turn in huge plays. Brown played exactly the same way. When he was in the NFL, run-heavy offenses were the norm. But that made Brown's accomplishments even more impressive. Every opponent knew he was coming at them, and he was still too big and too powerful to bring down. Had he not retired early, in the prime of his career, to pursue an acting career in Hollywood—his big break came in 1967 in a World War II film, *The Dirty Dozen*—Brown might have owned every major career rushing record.

RICHARD SHERMAN
Cornerback

HEIGHT, WEIGHT
6' 3", 195 pounds

TEAM
Seahawks

CAREER STATS
INT: 30
FUMBLES RECOVERED:
4 (six seasons)

AWARDS AND HONORS
Four-time Pro Bowler,
three-time first-team All-Pro,
2013 interceptions leader

Sherman and Hayes have four things in common: size, strength, sure hands, and greatness. Sherman has a reputation as one of the biggest, baddest cornerbacks in football. He sometimes lines up off the line of scrimmage, but he's known for smothering receivers at the line when he plays tight press coverage. He also has a reputation for bending the rules when it comes to holding receivers downfield but isn't flagged often. Hayes was famous for (or, as far as wide receivers were concerned, infamous for) his physical, bump-and-run coverage. During his playing career, the rules allowed defenders

LESTER HAYES
Cornerback

HEIGHT, WEIGHT
6' 0", 200 pounds

TEAM
Raiders

CAREER STATS
INT: 39
FUMBLES RECOVERED:
7 (10 seasons)

AWARDS AND HONORS
1980 NFL Defensive Player of the
Year, five-time Pro Bowler,
1980 interceptions leader

to physically manhandle receivers downfield. Hayes not only stifled pass catchers at the line of scrimmage, but he also had a reputation for roughing them up away from it. And he was known for having sticky hands. Literally. Many receivers rubbed a substance called Stickum on their hands in the 1970s. Hayes covered his hands, arms, and even jersey in the substance to help him hang onto interceptions. In fact, when the league banned Stickum in 1981, the edict was commonly referred to as the Lester Hayes Rule. Sherman, who was a wide receiver at Stanford University, has some of the surest hands ever for a defensive back. One other thing both these stars have in common: Quarterbacks have rarely tested them.

The
CURRENT
GUY

EARL THOMAS

Safety

HEIGHT, WEIGHT
5' 10", 202 pounds

TEAM
Seahawks

CAREER STATS
INT: 23
FUMBLES RECOVERED: 5
(seven seasons)

AWARDS AND HONORS
Five-time Pro Bowler,
four-time first-team All-Pro

In football, the free safety is the last line of defense, responsible for preventing big plays in the passing game. But the best free safeties are also capable of making big plays themselves. Thomas is the ultimate playmaker at safety. He is the anchor of Seattle's vaunted Legion of Boom secondary, a unit against which few opposing offenses try to throw deep. The same was true of quarterbacks when Reed was in the game. Along with being fast and athletic, Reed had a knack for reading the QB's eyes and making a break on passes from sideline to sideline. He had those instincts—and the sure hands of a wide receiver, leading the NFL in interceptions

ED REED
Safety

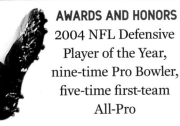

The OLD GUY

HEIGHT, WEIGHT
5' 11", 200 pounds

TEAMS
Ravens, Texans, Jets

CAREER STATS
INT: 64
FUMBLES RECOVERED: 13 (12 seasons)

AWARDS AND HONORS
2004 NFL Defensive Player of the Year, nine-time Pro Bowler, five-time first-team All-Pro

three times during his career. He even ran like an offensive player once the ball was in his hands. Reed scored nine touchdowns off interceptions or fumble recoveries during his career, including two returns of more than 100 yards. And he wasn't just a coverage player. Reed also had a well-earned reputation as a fierce hitter in the open field. Like Reed, Thomas has shown the ability to jump routes in the middle of the field and make plays from sideline to sideline. And while his Seahawks teammate Kam Chancellor is known as one of the most intimidating players at safety, Thomas has also earned a reputation for laying big hits on receivers who enter his area.

LUKE KUECHLY
Linebacker

HEIGHT, WEIGHT
6' 3", 238 pounds

TEAM
Panthers

CAREER STATS
INT: 12
FUMBLES RECOVERED: 5 (five seasons)

AWARDS AND HONORS
2013 NFL Defensive Player of the Year,
four-time Pro Bowler, three-time
first-team All-Pro, 2012 NFL
Defensive Rookie of the Year

The middle linebacker is like the quarterback of the defense, a coach on the field who makes sure everyone gets lined up before the snap. But the best middle linebackers are able to do much more after the play starts. Kuechly shows incredible instincts and the pure speed to close quickly once he sees where the ball is going. Lambert was the same way. He was the best at his position because he could quickly read and react to run plays. That ability—combined with his quickness and toughness—allowed him to stop run plays almost as soon as

JACK LAMBERT
Linebacker

The OLD GUY

HEIGHT, WEIGHT
6' 4", 220 pounds

TEAM
Steelers

CAREER STATS
INT: 28
FUMBLES RECOVERED: 17 (11 seasons)

AWARDS AND HONORS
1976 NFL Defensive Player of the Year, nine-time Pro Bowler, six-time first-team All-Pro, 1974 NFL Defensive Rookie of the Year

the running back took the handoff. But while Lambert is best remembered for bone-crushing hits (and, of course, his toothless grin), he was one of the best linebackers of all time when it came to pass coverage. He anchored the Steelers' Cover 2 zone defense, meaning he often had to defend passes deep over the middle. He was as good at that as any linebacker. In today's game, nobody covers the middle better than Kuechly, whose range matches that of defensive backs who are 40 pounds lighter.

JULIO JONES

Wide Receiver

HEIGHT, WEIGHT
6' 3", 220 pounds

TEAM
Falcons

CAREER STATS
REC: 497 **YDS:** 7,610 **TD:** 40
(six seasons)

AWARDS AND HONORS
Four-time Pro Bowler, two-time first-team
All Pro, 2015 NFL leader in receptions
and receiving yards

There are, for the most part, two kinds of receivers in professional football—those who are big and slow, and those who are small and fast. These two break the mold. Many thought the Falcons were crazy for offering a king's ransom (five picks!) to trade up and draft a nonquarterback, which they did in 2011 to take Jones. But the former Alabama receiver has proved to be unstoppable downfield. Since Jones entered the NFL in 2011, his 70 big-play catches (25 or more yards) are tied for second in the league. Moss, a two-time All-America

RANDY MOSS

Wide Receiver

HEIGHT, WEIGHT
6' 4", 215 pounds

TEAMS
Vikings,
Raiders, Patriots, Titans, 49ers

CAREER STATS
REC: 982 **YDS:** 15,292 **TD:** 156
(14 seasons)

AWARDS AND HONORS
Four-time first-team All Pro, five-time NFL
leader in TD catches, single-season record
for TD catches (23, in 2007)

at Marshall University, was considered one of
the greatest physical talents ever to step onto
a football field, but he slipped all the way to the
21st pick of the 1998 draft. Once his NFL career
began, he immediately became a dominant
playmaker for the Vikings. Not only could Moss
get downfield in a hurry, but he also became a
regular on highlight shows for his ability to
acrobatically adjust and make catches with
defenders all over him. After a rough stretch
with the Raiders, many thought Moss was
washed up. He was traded to the Patriots and
recaptured his magic in a record-setting season
with Tom Brady in 2007. Since the NFL started
tracking big plays receiving in 1994, no one has
more than Moss's 161.

The
CURRENT

ROB GRONKOWSKI
Tight End

HEIGHT, WEIGHT
6' 6", 265 pounds

TEAM
Patriots

CAREER STATS
REC: 405 **YDS:** 6,095 **TD:** 68
(seven seasons)

AWARDS AND HONORS
Three-time first-team
All-Pro, single-season
record for TDs by a tight
end (17, in 2011)

Gronkowski and Ditka: two tight ends who were big pass catchers with even bigger personalities. They have plenty in common: rare size and toughness, athleticism, and playmaking skills. Gronkowski is the most dangerous receiver among tight ends, demanding double teams and still turning in big gains. But he is also a big part of the Patriots' running game, overwhelming defensive backs who had assumed they'd be covering him on a pass play. Ditka was the NFL's first great big-play tight end. When he came to the Bears as a first-round pick out of the University of Pittsburgh in 1961, the typical tight end was asked to block and occasionally sneak out for a short reception. Make no mistake: Ditka could dish out crushing blocks. But he also changed everything in the passing game, running downfield for big

MIKE DITKA
Tight End

HEIGHT, WEIGHT
6' 2", 228 pounds

TEAMS
Bears, Eagles, Cowboys

CAREER STATS
REC: 427 **YDS**: 5,812 **TD**: 43
(12 seasons)

AWARDS AND HONORS
Two-time first-team All-Pro,
NFL 75th
Anniversary Team

gains like a wide receiver. For
the first time, defenses had to
come up with a specific game
plan to stop a tight end, much like
they do today against Gronkowski.
Off the field, Gronk is just as famous
for his goofy personality. Ditka, known
as Iron Mike, went on to become a
Super Bowl–winning coach for the
brash Bears teams of the 1980s.
His sweater, aviator sunglasses,
mustache, and permanent
scowl combined to make him
a unique sideline presence,
one still revered in
Chicago 30 years later.

TYRON SMITH
Offensive Tackle

HEIGHT, WEIGHT
6' 5", 320 pounds

TEAM
Cowboys

AWARDS AND HONORS
Four-time Pro Bowler, two-time first-team All-Pro

E verybody knows that the most important offensive position is quarterback. But most football coaches will tell you that the second most important position is the guy responsible for protecting the QB. That would be the man on the blind side, the left tackle. Smith is massive but almost impossibly athletic for a man his size. His blocking helped rookie running back Ezekiel Elliott win the 2016 NFL rushing title. Muñoz was one of the all-time greats at the position. Playing for the Bengals' fast-paced, high-scoring offense in the 1980s, Muñoz was responsible for protecting two NFL MVPs: Ken Anderson in 1981 and Boomer Esiason in 1988. The key to the tackle's game was

ANTHONY MUÑOZ

Offensive Tackle

HEIGHT, WEIGHT
6' 6", 278 pounds

TEAM
Bengals

AWARDS AND HONORS
Eleven-time Pro Bowler, nine-time first-team All-Pro,
NFL 75th Anniversary Team, NFL 1980s All-Decade Team

his rare blend of size and athleticism. Muñoz, who weighed nearly 300 pounds, was capable of pushing defenders out of the way as a run blocker. But he was amazingly fit for a big guy. He had little body fat, and his natural agility allowed him to stay in front of and stifle pass rushers. Smith plays the same role, and at the same level, as Muñoz once did.

The CURRENT

ODELL BECKHAM JR.
Wide Receiver

HEIGHT, WEIGHT
5' 11", 198 pounds

TEAM
Giants

CAREER STATS
REC: 288 **YDS**: 4,122 **TD**: 35 (three seasons)

AWARDS AND HONORS
Two-time Pro Bowler,
2014 NFL Offensive Rookie
of the Year

W hen talking about speed, size, and strength in a wide receiver, it can be easy to overlook the most important part of being a pass catcher: the catching. Beckham has become known for his acrobatic one-handed catches and often spends pregame warmups practicing them. No one in NFL history had hands like Rice, though. He had a remarkable work ethic and famously trained to become a wideout by catching bricks! His hands weren't just reliable, however; they were also

JERRY RICE
Wide Receiver

HEIGHT, WEIGHT
6' 2", 200 pounds

TEAMS
49ers, Raiders, Seahawks

CAREER STATS
REC: 1,549 **YDS**: 22,895 **TD**: 197 (20 seasons)

AWARDS AND HONORS
1987 NFL MVP, 13-time Pro Bowler, 10-time first-team All-Pro, NFL 75th Anniversary Team, NFL All-Decade Team (1980s, 1990s)

incredibly strong. He could snag passes away from his body and rip them away from defenders. And no one has ever been better at turning short catches into long gains, a staple of the 49ers' West Coast offense. Beckham is in the neighborhood, though. Just as Rice did, he has the ability to catch short passes, accelerate, and simply outrun a group of would-be tacklers for long touchdowns. And Beckham also has very strong hands.

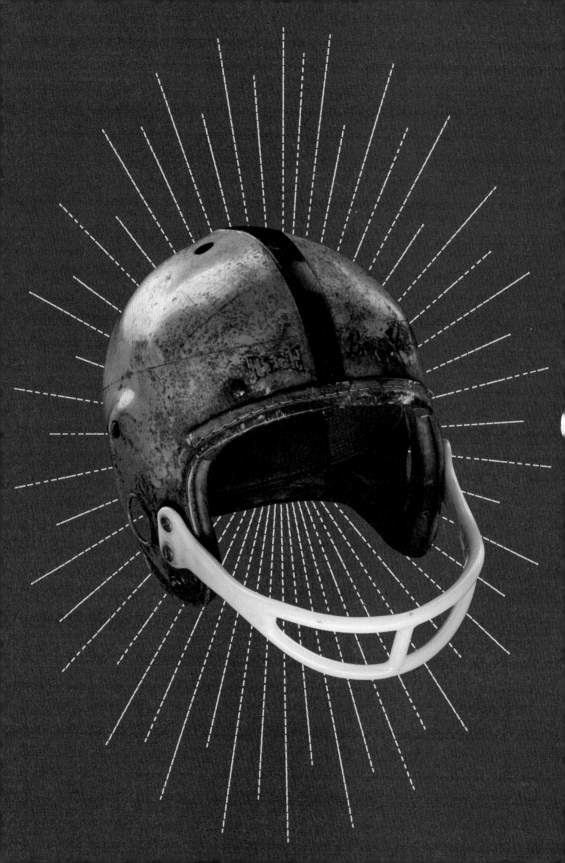

TEAM TIDBITS

A little bit of history, a dash of trivia, and an important nugget to help you get to know each of the 32 NFL teams better.

ARIZONA CARDINALS

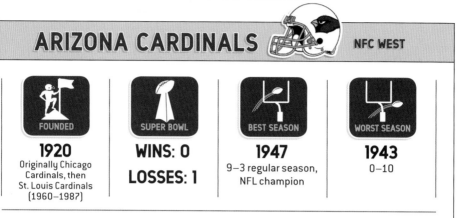

NFC WEST

FOUNDED	SUPER BOWL	BEST SEASON	WORST SEASON
1920	**WINS: 0**	**1947**	**1943**
Originally Chicago Cardinals, then St. Louis Cardinals (1960–1987)	**LOSSES: 1**	9–3 regular season, NFL champion	0–10

THE GREATS

Larry Wilson, Safety A Hall of Famer for the St. Louis Cardinals (1960–1972), Wilson later worked as a coach and in the front office.

Dan Dierdorf, Offensive Tackle This star blocker for St. Louis (1971–1983) made the Hall of Fame and found *additional* fame as a broadcaster.

Larry Fitzgerald, Wide Receiver The all-time great almost single-handedly carried Arizona to a Super Bowl title with a record-setting 2008 postseason. Fitzgerald caught 30 passes for 546 yards and seven touchdowns.

Charley Trippi, Quarterback–Halfback A Chicago Cardinals star as a runner, passer, receiver, and return man in the 1940s and 1950s, Trippi helped the Cardinals to their first title, in 1947.

GOOD TO KNOW

The greatest hero in Cardinals history played only four NFL seasons and was never named to a Pro Bowl. Pat Tillman, who played college football at nearby Arizona State University, might have become a star one day, but the rising young safety left professional football after only four seasons to join the military. He passed up a contract that was worth more than $3 million to fight the war on terrorism. A U.S. Army Ranger, Tillman was killed in 2004 while fighting in Afghanistan, when he was 27 years old. He was recognized as a hero for his sacrifice, and his number 40 jersey was retired by the Cardinals.

ATLANTA FALCONS

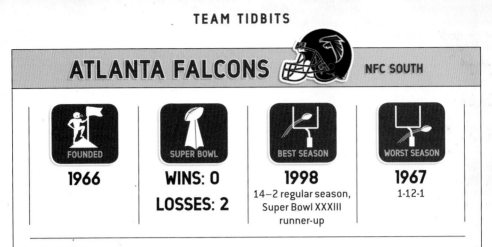

NFC SOUTH

FOUNDED	SUPER BOWL	BEST SEASON	WORST SEASON
1966	**WINS: 0** **LOSSES: 2**	**1998** 14–2 regular season, Super Bowl XXXIII runner-up	**1967** 1-12-1

THE GREATS

Claude Humphrey, Defensive End One of the most dominant pass rushers of his era, Humphrey made the Pro Bowl five straight seasons, from 1970 through 1974.

Tommy Nobis, Linebacker Known as Mr. Falcon, he was the first player drafted in team history. The linebacker was a five-time Pro Bowler in the late 1960s and 1970s.

Steve Bartkowski, Quarterback A good quarterback on some bad Falcons teams, Bartkowski led the NFL in touchdown passes in 1980.

Julio Jones, Wide Receiver One of the truly dynamic players of the modern era, Jones led the league in receiving yards in 2015.

GOOD TO KNOW

The Falcons have always earned an "A" when it comes to attitude. Atlanta has been home to some of the brashest players in NFL history. There was Deion Sanders *(right)*, better known as Neon Deion or Prime Time. During his five seasons with the Falcons, the outspoken cornerback was famous for his shutdown play and for his high-stepping end zone dances when returning interceptions and punts. In 1998, the Falcons made their first run to the Super Bowl. The team invented a new celebration, a dance called the Dirty Bird, which involved arms flapping up and down and elbows flying.

BALTIMORE RAVENS — AFC NORTH

FOUNDED
1996
Originally Cleveland
Browns, 1946–1995

SUPER BOWL
WINS: 2
LOSSES: 0

BEST SEASON
2000
12–4 regular season,
Super Bowl XXXV
champion

WORST SEASON
1996
4–12

THE GREATS

Ray Lewis, Linebacker Arguably the greatest linebacker of all time, Lewis was a 13-time Pro Bowler who won two Super Bowls.

Joe Flacco, Quarterback The only true franchise QB the Ravens have ever had, Flacco was named the 2008 Rookie of the Year and MVP of Super Bowl XLVII.

John Harbaugh, Coach He took over a team in 2008 that was 5–11 the year before and went on to lead the Ravens to at least one playoff win (including Super Bowl XLVII) in six of his first seven seasons.

Ed Reed, Safety Often overshadowed by Lewis, Reed was an all-time great in his own right, one of football's most feared safeties during the 2000s.

GOOD TO KNOW

The NFL didn't have much in common with great writers of the 19th century. Until the Ravens came around in the 1990s, that is. When the Browns announced they would relocate to Baltimore from Cleveland for the 1996 season, part of the agreement was that the Browns' "team history" would remain in Cleveland. So instead of becoming the Baltimore Browns, the team would need a whole new identity. More than 30,000 fans suggested new names, and the franchise settled on the Ravens. Why? Writer Edgar Allen Poe *(right)* lived and worked in Baltimore. His most famous work was a poem titled *The Raven*.

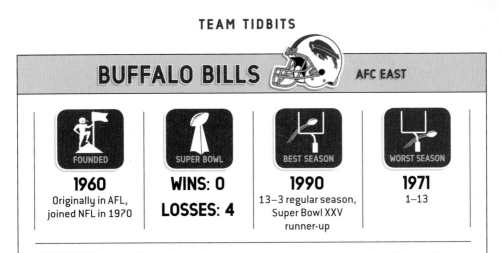

BUFFALO BILLS

AFC EAST

FOUNDED	SUPER BOWL	BEST SEASON	WORST SEASON
1960	**WINS: 0**	**1990**	**1971**
Originally in AFL, joined NFL in 1970	**LOSSES: 4**	13–3 regular season, Super Bowl XXV runner-up	1–13

THE GREATS

Jim Kelly, Quarterback Kelly led Buffalo's unstoppable K-Gun offense in the 1990s, putting up monster numbers while taking the Bills to four straight AFC titles.

Bruce Smith, Defensive End The only man in NFL history to record 200 career sacks (a stat that became official in 1982) was an 11-time Pro Bowler in the 1980s and 1990s.

Thurman Thomas, Running Back One of the game's great all-purpose backs, he was named to the NFL's 1990s All-Decade Team and was league MVP in 1991.

Andre Reed, Wide Receiver This Hall of Fame receiver was Jim Kelly's go-to wideout during the Bills' heyday, making the Pro Bowl seven times.

GOOD TO KNOW

The Bills were oh-so-close in their first Super Bowl. After a back-and-forth battle, they trailed the Giants 20–19 and had the ball at their own 10-yard line with 2:16 left. Jim Kelly *(right)* led a masterly drive. Kicker Scott Norwood set up for a potential game-winning field goal from 47 yards out, but the kick sailed wide right. It was a heartbreaking loss. Little did the Bills know, they'd return to the big game in each of the next three years! But none of those games were nearly as close as the first. The Bills are the only team in NFL history to make it to four straight Super Bowls, yet they still don't have a win to show for it.

CAROLINA PANTHERS

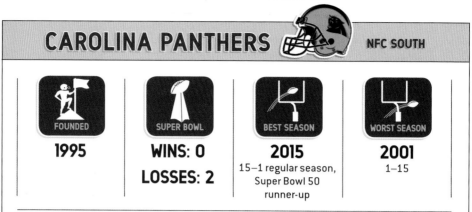

NFC SOUTH

FOUNDED	SUPER BOWL	BEST SEASON	WORST SEASON
1995	WINS: 0 LOSSES: 2	2015 15–1 regular season, Super Bowl 50 runner-up	2001 1–15

THE GREATS

Cam Newton, Quarterback The top pick of the 2011 draft was the 2015 league MVP. Newton has led the Panthers on their most sustained run of success.

Steve Smith, Wide Receiver This undersized wideout's toughness made him unstoppable in his prime. Smith led the NFL in receiving yards and TDs in 2005.

Sam Mills, Linebacker Mills led the Panthers in their early years and then as an assistant coach. His Keep Pounding motto is still used by the team.

Jordan Gross, Offensive Tackle A rock at left tackle, Gross made three Pro Bowls and started 167 games from 2003 through 2013.

GOOD TO KNOW

They're one of the NFL's newest teams, but the Panthers have already had their fill of drama. They've made the Super Bowl twice, each time after a season in which they had a losing record. And for that second Super Bowl trip, they were led by Cam Newton *(right)*, arguably the most exciting player of the modern era. An unusual quarterback (in that he's 245 pounds and capable of moving like a running back), Newton elevated his passing skills during the 2015 season. He led the Panthers to a 15–1 regular season and won the franchise's first-ever league MVP award. He also became a true superstar, celebrated for his skills, his style, and his winning smile.

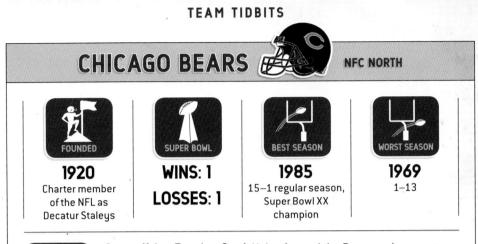

CHICAGO BEARS

NFC NORTH

FOUNDED
1920
Charter member
of the NFL as
Decatur Staleys

SUPER BOWL
WINS: 1
LOSSES: 1

BEST SEASON
1985
15–1 regular season,
Super Bowl XX
champion

WORST SEASON
1969
1–13

THE GREATS

George Halas, Founder–Coach Halas formed the Bears and was a star player and six-time championship coach.

Walter Payton, Running Back Many call the 1977 MVP, who was known as Sweetness, the greatest running back of all time.

Dick Butkus, Linebacker One of football's most feared hitters made the Pro Bowl in eight of nine years. Butkus was also on NFL All-Decade teams for the 1960s and 1970s.

Mike Ditka, Tight End–Coach An all-time great as a player, Ditka went on to win NFL Coach of the Year twice. He coached the Bears to their only Super Bowl title.

GOOD TO KNOW

When discussing the greatest teams of all time, many simply award the title to the 1972 Dolphins, the only team in the Super Bowl era to go undefeated. But a closer look reveals an argument for the 1985 Bears. That Chicago team had a cast of stars on defense and legendary running back Walter Payton leading the offense. The Bears were so confident in their ability to dominate that the team recorded a celebratory rap song, "The Super Bowl Shuffle," three months before the big game. Under the guidance of Mike Ditka *(right)*, Chicago went 15–1, shut out its first two postseason opponents (the Giants and the Los Angeles Rams), then went on to demolish the Patriots 46–10 in Super Bowl XX.

CINCINNATI BENGALS

AFC NORTH

FOUNDED
1968
Originally in AFL,
joined NFL in 1970

SUPER BOWL
WINS: 0
LOSSES: 2

BEST SEASON
1988
12—4 regular season,
Super Bowl XXIII
runner-up

WORST SEASON
2002
2–14

THE GREATS

Anthony Muñoz, Offensive Tackle An 11-time Pro Bowl left tackle, Muñoz is considered the greatest O-lineman of all time.

Ken Anderson, Quarterback He led the Bengals to their first Super Bowl in 1981, when he was NFL MVP.

Paul Brown, Coach Better known for his time in Cleveland, Brown co-founded the Bengals and won two UPI Coach of the Year awards in Cincinnati.

Boomer Esiason, Quarterback Esiason was a four-time Pro Bowler who led Cincy's no-huddle offense in the late 1980s and led the NFL in passer rating in 1988.

GOOD TO KNOW

Fast-paced, high-scoring offenses are the norm these days, but they weren't in the 1980s. That's what made the 1988 Bengals such a revolutionary team.

Under coach Sam Wyche, quarterback Boomer Esiason pioneered the no-huddle, hurry-up offense to catch defenses off-guard. The Bengals, who had won only four games the previous season, improved to 12–4 while leading the NFL in points (28.0) and total yards per game (378.6). The offense also made a star out of running back Ickey Woods (right), whose trademark Ickey Shuffle touchdown dance swept the nation. The Bengals nearly won Super Bowl XXIII, falling only when 49ers QB Joe Montana led a comeback in the final minute.

CLEVELAND BROWNS

AFC NORTH

FOUNDED	SUPER BOWL	BEST SEASON	WORST SEASON
1946	**WINS: 0**	**1950**	**2016**
Joined NFL in 1950, relocated to Baltimore in 1996, reestablished in 1999	**LOSSES: 0**	10–2 regular season, NFL champions	1–15

Paul Brown, Coach Considered by many to be the greatest NFL coach of all time, the team is named after him.

Jim Brown, Running Back This dominant runner won eight rushing titles and four MVP awards in the 1950s and 1960s before retiring.

Otto Graham, Quarterback The Hall of Fame signal-caller led the Browns to an NFL title game every year of his career (1946 through 1955), winning seven championships.

Lou Groza, Offensive Tackle–Kicker Groza played 21 seasons in Cleveland during the 1940s, 1950s, and 1960s, making nine Pro Bowls and winning eight titles.

Cleveland might have the most famous fan base in sports. Known as the Dawg Pound, those who sit in the end zone bleachers at FirstEnergy Stadium wear dog masks, a tradition that started with the Browns' Dawgs defense of the mid-1980s. (A cornerback gave his defensive teammates the nickname.) Browns fans are also known for having to suffer through heartbreaking defeats and many losing seasons. Cleveland is the only NFL city to have never participated in or hosted a Super Bowl. Before the Super Bowl era, however, the Browns won four titles in the All-America Football Conference and four more after joining the NFL. Their eight championships are more than any other AFC team.

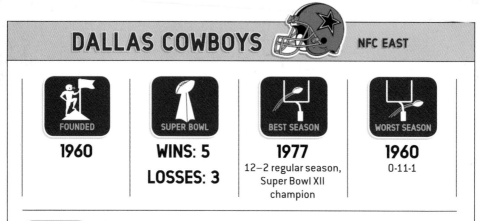

DALLAS COWBOYS — NFC EAST

FOUNDED	SUPER BOWL	BEST SEASON	WORST SEASON
1960	WINS: 5 LOSSES: 3	1977 12–2 regular season, Super Bowl XII champion	1960 0-11-1

THE GREATS

Emmitt Smith, Running Back The NFL's all-time leading rusher helped Dallas to three Super Bowl victories in the 1990s. He was league MVP in 1993 and earned four NFL rushing titles over his career.

Roger Staubach, Quarterback Staubach was a Hall of Fame player who led Dallas to two Super Bowls with a scrambling, big-play style.

Tom Landry, Coach This pioneering, defense-first coach led the Cowboys to their first two Super Bowl victories.

Troy Aikman, Quarterback Aikman's efficient game and leadership ability highlighted the Cowboys' three Super Bowl–winning teams of the 1990s. The Hall of Famer was named Walter Payton Man of the Year in 1997.

GOOD TO KNOW

There has never been a more steady presence for an NFL franchise than Tom Landry was for Dallas. As an assistant coach in the 1950s, Landry pioneered the 4–3 defense, an alignment still used in the league today. He was hired as the Cowboys' first coach, for the 1960 season, and his stoic demeanor, suit and tie, and trademark fedora hat made him a distinctive presence on the sideline. He turned the expansion Cowboys into a football power, leading them to five Super Bowl appearances, including wins in Super Bowls VI and XII. Landry stayed in Dallas until 1988; his 29 consecutive seasons at the helm are tied for a record for an NFL coach.

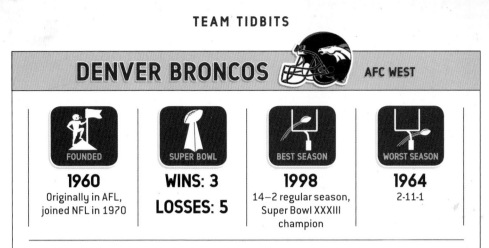

DENVER BRONCOS

AFC WEST

FOUNDED	SUPER BOWL	BEST SEASON	WORST SEASON
1960	**WINS: 3**	**1998**	**1964**
Originally in AFL, joined NFL in 1970	**LOSSES: 5**	14–2 regular season, Super Bowl XXXIII champion	2-11-1

THE GREATS

John Elway, Quarterback This QB had one of the strongest arms the NFL has ever seen. A member of the 1990s All-Decade Team, Elway led Denver to five Super Bowl appearances and two victories and was MVP of the 1987 season.

Shannon Sharpe, Tight End One of the greatest pass-catching tight ends to ever play, Sharpe made seven of his eight Pro Bowls while playing for Denver.

Floyd Little, Running Back The Hall of Famer carried the team through the early years. Despite a lack of talent around him, he was a three-time Pro Bowler and two-time AFL All-Star.

Terrell Davis, Running Back Injuries limited him to seven seasons, but he is a Hall of Famer. He was the 1998 NFL MVP, a three-time All-Pro, and Super Bowl XXXII MVP.

GOOD TO KNOW

John Elway was drafted by the Baltimore Colts with the first pick in the 1983 draft, but he said he'd rather play baseball (he had been a New York Yankees draft pick) than suit up for the Colts. So they traded him to Denver. Elway made the Broncos contenders and led them to three Super Bowls in four years in the late 1980s. (The Broncos lost all three.) He returned to the Big Game in 1997 and led Denver to the first of back-to-back titles. He was MVP of Super Bowl XXXIII, then retired. After leaving football for a few years, he returned to the Broncos as general manager in 2011. The team he built won Super Bowl 50, giving Elway a third championship ring.

DETROIT LIONS — NFC NORTH

FOUNDED	SUPER BOWL	BEST SEASON	WORST SEASON
1930	**WINS: 0**	**1953**	**2008**
As Portsmouth Spartans. Became Lions in 1934	**LOSSES: 0**	10–2 regular season, NFL champion	0–16

THE GREATS

Barry Sanders, Running Back The most dynamic runner in NFL history rushed for 1,000 yards and made the Pro Bowl in each of his 10 seasons. If he hadn't retired when he did, he might have set every major NFL career rushing record.

Bobby Layne, Quarterback–Kicker Layne, a six-time Pro Bowl passer, led the Lions to two NFL titles and was a member of the 1950s All-Decade Team.

Joe Schmidt, Linebacker This Hall of Famer was a 10-time All-Pro and member of the 1950s NFL All-Decade Team, helping the Lions to two championships.

Calvin Johnson, Wide Receiver One of the most physically imposing athletes to ever play in the NFL, Johnson made the Pro Bowl six times and holds the all-time single-season record for receiving yards (1,964 in 2012).

GOOD TO KNOW

In Week 5 of the 2008 season, the Lions led the Vikings 10–9 with less than five minutes to go. But Minnesota put together a late drive, and a last-second field goal by Ryan Longwell made Detroit's record 0–5 in the still-young season. Had the Lions held on for that win, they'd be remembered as a very bad team but not a historically bad one: The 2008 Lions wouldn't come that close to victory the rest of the season. While there have been other winless streaks in pro football, the Lions were the first (and, through 2016, still only) team to lose every matchup in a 16-game season.

GREEN BAY PACKERS

NFC NORTH

FOUNDED	SUPER BOWL	BEST SEASON	WORST SEASON
1919 Joined NFL in 1921	**WINS: 4** **LOSSES: 1**	**1962** 13–1 regular season, NFL champion	**1958** 1-10-1

THE GREATS

Bart Starr, Quarterback This iconic QB didn't put up the biggest stats in Green Bay's run-driven offense, but he led the Pack to five NFL titles, including victories in Super Bowls I and II.

Vince Lombardi, Coach Arguably the greatest coach of all time, Lombardi led the Packers to five NFL titles and won 90% of his postseason games.

Don Hutson, Split End One of the NFL's first superstar playmakers, Hutson led the NFL in receiving yardage seven times during the 1930s and 1940s. He was league MVP in 1941 and 1942.

Brett Favre, Quarterback The Hall of Famer known as a gunslinger for his strong arm and willingness to take big risks was a three-time NFL MVP and 11-time Pro Bowler.

GOOD TO KNOW

Vince Lombardi was so successful as the Packers' head coach that the trophy awarded to the Super Bowl winner is named after him. A five-time NFL champion with the Packers, Lombardi was famous for his locker-room speeches and motivational techniques, but he was also a brilliant football mind. He engineered one of the most unstoppable plays in football history, a sweep that was often designed for fullback Jim Taylor. It eventually became known as the Lombardi Sweep. He stepped down as Packers coach after the 1967 season, then took over the Redskins in 1969. Lombardi only coached one season in Washington before dying of cancer at 57.

HOUSTON TEXANS

AFC SOUTH

FOUNDED	SUPER BOWL	BEST SEASON	WORST SEASON
2002	**WINS: 0** **LOSSES: 0**	**2012** 12–4 regular season, division champion	**2013** 2–14

THE GREATS

J.J. Watt, Defensive Lineman Early in his career, Watt established himself as one of the most dominant players the game has ever seen. He is the only player in NFL history with two 20-sack seasons, and he is a three-time league Defensive Player of the Year.

Andre Johnson, Wide Receiver This supersized wideout made the Pro Bowl seven times during 12 seasons in Houston and led the NFL in receiving yards in 2008 and 2009.

Arian Foster, Running Back Foster went undrafted in 2009, then made four Pro Bowls. He won the NFL rushing title in 2010 and was the rushing TD leader in 2010 and 2012.

Mario Williams, Defensive End The first pick of the 2006 draft became one of the league's most feared pass rushers, with 14 sacks in 2007 and 12 more in 2008.

GOOD TO KNOW

The Texans are the babies of the NFL. They're the league's newest franchise, but they're not the first NFL team Houston has ever had. The Oilers were Houston's first pro football franchise, playing from 1960 through 1996 before relocating to Nashville, Tennessee. (They're now the Titans.) In 2000, the expansion franchise announced a nickname search that narrowed to five choices: Apollos, Bobcats, Stallions, Texans, and Wildcatters. Texans won, though the team actually had to get the naming rights from the Kansas City Chiefs. The Chiefs were originally known as the Dallas Texans before moving to Kansas.

INDIANAPOLIS COLTS

AFC SOUTH

FOUNDED
1953
As Baltimore Colts.
Moved to Indianapolis
in 1984

SUPER BOWL
WINS: 2
LOSSES: 2

BEST SEASON
1970
11-2-1 regular
season, Super Bowl V
champion

WORST SEASON
1982
0-8-1

Johnny Unitas, Quarterback Unitas won four NFL MVP awards, made 10 Pro Bowls, and was a member of the NFL 75th Anniversary Team.

Marvin Harrison, Wide Receiver Peyton Manning's go-to guy was an eight-time Pro Bowler who set the single-season mark for catches (143 in 2002).

Peyton Manning, Quarterback He single-handedly made the Colts a Super Bowl contender in the 2000s. The No. 1 pick of the 1998 draft won four NFL MVPs and made 11 Pro Bowls in 13 seasons with the team. He was named Super Bowl XLI MVP.

Raymond Berry, Wide Receiver One of the greatest playmakers in NFL history, Berry made six Pro Bowls and led the NFL in receiving three times (1957, 1959, 1960).

Johnny Unitas was a quarterback ahead of his time. The NFL was much different during the 1950s and 1960s, Unitas's prime. Unlike today, defenders could make contact with receivers well downfield, and many teams found running the ball to be much more efficient. The Colts were different because of Unitas. Wearing his famous black high-top cleats, Johnny U was a maestro when it came to manipulating defenses. With the passing game leading the way, the Colts won NFL titles in 1958 and 1959, then added a Super Bowl V title after the 1970 season. Unitas led the NFL in passing yards four times and in TD passes four straight years, from 1957 through 1960.

JACKSONVILLE JAGUARS

AFC SOUTH

FOUNDED	SUPER BOWL	BEST SEASON	WORST SEASON
1995	**WINS: 0** **LOSSES: 0**	**1999** 14–2, division champion	**2012** 2–14

THE GREATS

Tony Boselli, Offensive Tackle The first-ever draft pick for the Jaguars (second overall in 1995), Boselli made five Pro Bowls in seven seasons with Jacksonville before injuries cut his career short.

Mark Brunell, Quarterback Jacksonville's first franchise QB made three Pro Bowls and led the Jaguars to the playoffs from 1996 through 1999.

Fred Taylor, Running Back This workhorse spent 11 seasons in Jacksonville, rushing for 1,000 yards seven times.

Maurice Jones–Drew, Running Back Jones-Drew was a diminutive player (5' 7") who was one of the league's best all-around backs in his prime. He made three straight Pro Bowls (2009 through 2011) and won the 2011 NFL rushing crown.

GOOD TO KNOW

The Jaguars joined the NFL as an expansion team in 1995. The hardest thing for any new team is building a roster. And the hardest player for any team to find is a franchise quarterback. The Jaguars had a good feeling about Mark Brunell *(right)*, who was the backup in Green Bay, and they traded two draft picks to bring him in as their first QB. A lefthanded passer with a flair for making plays, Brunell led the Jags to almost instant success. The team went to the playoffs in 1996, just its second season in existence, and made it all the way to the AFC title game. Jacksonville would make the playoffs in each of the next three seasons.

KANSAS CITY CHIEFS

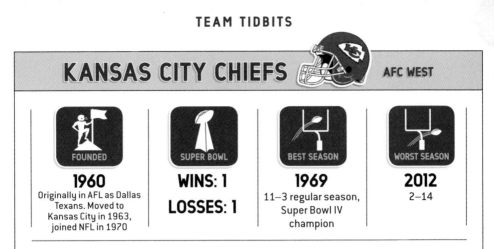

AFC WEST

FOUNDED	SUPER BOWL	BEST SEASON	WORST SEASON
1960	**WINS: 1**	**1969**	**2012**
Originally in AFL as Dallas Texans. Moved to Kansas City in 1963, joined NFL in 1970	**LOSSES: 1**	11–3 regular season, Super Bowl IV champion	2–14

THE GREATS

Len Dawson, Quarterback This Hall of Fame QB was a six-time AFL All-Star and MVP of Super Bowl IV.

Derrick Thomas, Linebacker One of the game's most feared pass rushers, the nine-time Pro Bowler still holds the league single-game sacks record (seven, in a 1990 matchup against Seattle). Thomas was on the NFL's All-Decade Team for the 1990s.

Hank Stram, Coach The first coach in franchise history made the Hall of Fame after leading the team to three AFL titles and a victory in Super Bowl IV.

Willie Lanier, Linebacker Lanier was a dominating presence in the late 1960s and 1970s. The Hall of Famer was All-AFL twice and a six-time NFL Pro Bowler.

GOOD TO KNOW

The Chiefs were the last American Football League power. As the AFL and the NFL neared their 1970 merger, it was Kansas City that dominated the upstart league. Behind QB Len Dawson *(right)* and Hall of Fame coach Hank Stram, the Chiefs won two of the last four AFL titles. They had lost the first NFL-AFL championship game (later called Super Bowl I) to the Packers after the 1966 season. In the Super Bowl after the 1969 season, Kansas City was considered a heavy underdog against the Vikings. But Dawson led the way for the offense, and a dominating performance by the D gave the team a 23–7 victory and the franchise its first (and only) Super Bowl title.

LOS ANGELES CHARGERS

AFC WEST

FOUNDED
1960
Originally in AFL as L.A. Chargers. Moved to San Diego in 1961, joined NFL in 1970, returned to L.A. in 2017

SUPER BOWL
WINS: 0
LOSSES: 1

BEST SEASON
1963
11–3 regular season, AFL champion

WORST SEASON
2000
1–15

THE GREATS

Junior Seau, Linebacker One of the greatest linebackers in NFL history was a Pro Bowler in 12 of his 13 seasons with the Chargers and the NFL Defensive Player of the Year in 1992.

Lance Alworth, Wide Receiver This premier playmaker in the 1960s was a seven-time AFL All-Star (1963 through 1969) and led the AFL in receiving yards and receiving TDs three times each.

LaDainian Tomlinson, Running Back The Hall of Famer was a two-time rushing leader (2006, 2007) and NFL MVP in 2006, when he scored a single-season-record 31 TDs.

Philip Rivers, Quarterback A cerebral passer, he has carried the offense through lean years. Rivers, a five-time Pro Bowler, led the NFL in passing yards in 2010.

GOOD TO KNOW

The Chargers' 41–38 victory in the scorching heat in Miami in January 1982 still stands as one of the most exciting games ever played. They jumped out to a 24–0 lead, only to have the Dolphins tie the game early in the second half. The teams traded TDs and headed to overtime, in which each side missed a short field goal before Rolf Benirschke's kick won it. The Chargers and Miami set combined records in points, total yards, and passing yards. Kellen Winslow, who caught 13 passes, famously needed to be helped to the locker room afterward *(right)*. The next week the Chargers lost the AFC title game in Cincinnati, where it was –9° with a –59° windchill!

LOS ANGELES RAMS

NFC WEST

FOUNDED
1937
As Cleveland Rams.
Moved to L.A. in 1946.
Also played in St. Louis
(1995–2015)

SUPER BOWL
WINS: 1
LOSSES: 2

BEST SEASON
1999
13–3 regular season,
Super Bowl XXXIV
champion

WORST SEASON
2009
1–15

THE GREATS

Deacon Jones, Defensive End The greatest pass rusher of all time played before sacks was an official stat. It is thought that he had as many as four 20-sack seasons during the era of 14-game schedules, including what would then have been a record 22 in 1968.

Eric Dickerson, Running Back Three of his four NFL rushing titles in the 1980s came while he was with the Rams, including the single-season rushing record (2,105 yards in 1984).

Jack Youngblood, Defensive End This intimidating pass rusher was a two-time Defensive Player of the Year (1975, 1976) and seven-time Pro Bowl selection.

Marshall Faulk, Running Back Faulk was an all-purpose star for the Greatest Show on Turf teams and won back-to-back NFL MVP awards (2000, 2001).

GOOD TO KNOW

It seems as if the Rams simply belong in Los Angeles. They first moved west from Cleveland in 1946, only to leave for St. Louis after the 1994 season. They couldn't stay away, though, relocating to L.A. for a second time, before the 2016 season. The Rams have a Hollywood connection: The 1978 film *Heaven Can Wait* is considered one of the best sports movies ever made. In it, Warren Beatty *(right)* stars as an L.A. Rams QB. The St. Louis Rams had a made-for-Hollywood story too. In 1999, backup QB Kurt Warner, who had worked at a grocery store and played in the Arena League, won NFL MVP and led the Rams to victory in Super Bowl XXXIV.

MIAMI DOLPHINS

AFC EAST

FOUNDED	SUPER BOWL	BEST SEASON	WORST SEASON
1966	**WINS: 2**	**1972**	**2007**
Originally in AFL, joined NFL in 1970	**LOSSES: 3**	14–0 regular season, Super Bowl VIII champion	1–15

Dan Marino, Quarterback Often referred to as the greatest football player to never win a title, Marino carried Miami through the 1980s and 1990s and was the 1984 NFL MVP, a nine-time Pro Bowler, and a five-time passing yardage leader.

Don Shula, Coach The all-time leader in career wins as a coach (328 regular season, 347 including playoffs) led Miami to five Super Bowls, including two wins.

Larry Csonka, Running Back This bruising runner made the Pro Bowl from 1970 through 1974 and was MVP of Super Bowl VIII (145 rushing yards and two TDs).

Bob Griese, Quarterback Griese led Miami's offense for those dominant 1970s teams. The Hall of Famer won two Super Bowls, made six Pro Bowls, and was NFL MVP in 1971.

During the Super Bowl era, which began in 1966, perfection has eluded every team—except for the 1972 Dolphins. Led by Don Shula, Miami ran through a 14–0 regular season, then won all three postseason games. The Dolphins' claim to the title Best Team Ever has been debated, considering Miami played an especially easy slate of regular-season games due to odd scheduling rules of the time. In another quirk, however, they had to play the Steelers in Pittsburgh in the postseason. (Not exactly friendly territory.) Whatever your opinion, the Dolphins do remain the only perfect team since the NFL and the AFL merged.

MINNESOTA VIKINGS

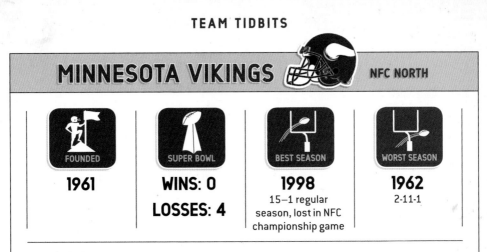

NFC NORTH

FOUNDED	SUPER BOWL	BEST SEASON	WORST SEASON
1961	**WINS: 0** **LOSSES: 4**	**1998** 15–1 regular season, lost in NFC championship game	**1962** 2-11-1

THE GREATS

Fran Tarkenton, Quarterback Known for his incredible playmaking ability, Tarkenton led the Vikings to three Super Bowls while making nine Pro Bowls during the 1960s and 1970s. He won NFL MVP in 1975.

Alan Page, Defensive Tackle The 1971 NFL Defensive Player of the Year and league MVP was the first defensive player (and one of only two) to be named NFL MVP by the Associated Press (1971).

Adrian Peterson, Running Back This powerful runner was NFL MVP in 2012, when he gained the second-most yards ever in a single season (2,097).

Cris Carter, Wide Receiver The Hall of Fame wideout made eight Pro Bowls in the 1990s and led the NFL in TD catches three times (1995, 1997, 1999).

GOOD TO KNOW

NFL teams often get tough when it comes to contract negotiations with players. But in 2015, the Vikings took a hard stance with their *mascot.* Ragnar was an actual person (real name: Joe Juranitch, *right*) with an enormous beard and a full Vikings costume. From 1994 to 2015, Ragnar was famous for taking the field on a motorcycle and trash talking opposing star players. But when he asked for a huge raise, the Vikings decided they were better off without him. After all, the team had introduced a costumed character, Viktor the Viking, in 2007. The last time Ragnar was seen, he was wearing a Packers cheesehead.

NEW ENGLAND PATRIOTS

AFC EAST

FOUNDED
1960
Originally in AFL as
Boston Patriots
(1960–1970), joined
NFL in 1970

SUPER BOWL
WINS: 5
LOSSES: 4

BEST SEASON
2004
14–2 regular season,
Super Bowl XXXIX
champion

WORST SEASON
1990
1–15

THE GREATS

Tom Brady, Quarterback The sixth-round pick in 2000 has become one of the greatest players in NFL history. Through the 2016 season, Brady was a two-time NFL MVP (2007, 2010), five-time Super Bowl champion, and four-time Super Bowl MVP.

Bill Belichick, Coach Belichick led the Patriots to seven Super Bowl appearances and five Super Bowl victories in his first 17 seasons leading the Patriots.

John Hannah, Guard Considered one of the greatest offensive linemen ever, Hannah made the All-Pro team in 10 consecutive seasons, from 1976 through 1985.

Adam Vinatieri, Kicker The NFL's all-time best clutch kicker connected on game-winning field goals in Super Bowls XXXVI and XXXVIII.

GOOD TO KNOW

The greatest coach-quarterback combination in NFL history came together by chance. The Patriots went 5–11 in 2000, their first season under Bill Belichick. They were 0–1 the next season when franchise quarterback Drew Bledsoe, just signed to a record $103 million contract, suffered a major injury in the second game. Belichick had to rely on an unknown second-year QB taken in the sixth round of the 2000 draft—Tom Brady. He turned New England's season around and led the hapless Pats to victory in Super Bowl XXXVI the next year. Since then, Belichick and Brady have won more games together than any coach-QB combo in NFL history.

NEW ORLEANS SAINTS

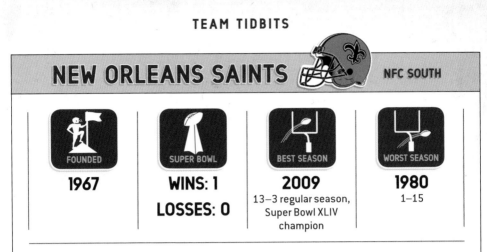

NFC SOUTH

FOUNDED	SUPER BOWL	BEST SEASON	WORST SEASON
1967	**WINS: 1** **LOSSES: 0**	**2009** 13–3 regular season, Super Bowl XLIV champion	**1980** 1–15

THE GREATS

Drew Brees, Quarterback Brees joined the Saints as a free agent before the 2006 season and was a two-time Offensive Player of the Year (2008, 2011) and Super Bowl XLIV MVP.

Willie Roaf, Offensive Tackle He made the Pro Bowl in seven of his nine seasons with the Saints (1993 through 2001). The Hall of Famer was a member of the NFL's 1990s and 2000s All-Decade teams.

Rickey Jackson, Linebacker The Hall of Fame pass rusher and six-time Pro Bowler is the franchise leader in sacks (115, from 1981 through 1993).

Archie Manning, Quarterback Also known as father of Peyton and Eli, this playmaking QB carried the Saints through the team's lean years in the 1970s, making two Pro Bowls.

GOOD TO KNOW

The most inspirational play in Saints history came on special teams. In 2005, the city of New Orleans was ravaged by Hurricane Katrina, which wiped out whole neighborhoods and forced the Saints to relocate to different stadiums. They returned to New Orleans for the 2006 season and hosted the Falcons on *Monday Night Football* in their first game back at the Superdome. The Saints took control early when Steve Gleason blocked a punt that was returned for a touchdown, setting the tone in the emotional win. Gleason would become an inspiration beyond football, making his battle against ALS public and advocating for more research into the disease.

NEW YORK GIANTS

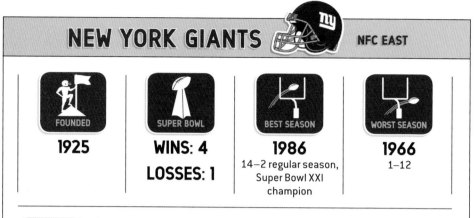

NFC EAST

FOUNDED	SUPER BOWL	BEST SEASON	WORST SEASON
1925	**WINS: 4** **LOSSES: 1**	**1986** 14–2 regular season, Super Bowl XXI champion	**1966** 1–12

THE GREATS

Lawrence Taylor, Linebacker The talented but troubled Hall of Famer is considered one of the greatest edge pass rushers of all time. He's one of two defensive players to ever win NFL MVP honors (1986).

Eli Manning, Quarterback Manning, the top pick of the 2004 draft, became a four-time Pro Bowler and two-time Super Bowl MVP (XLII and XLVI).

Frank Gifford, Halfback–Wide Receiver One of the top playmakers of the 1950s and an eight-time Pro Bowler, Gifford won NFL MVP and led the Giants to the NFL title in 1956.

Y.A. Tittle, Quarterback Tittle only played four seasons with the Giants, and he won NFL MVP in three of those (1961 through 1963).

GOOD TO KNOW

In Super Bowl XLII, New York faced the Patriots, who were trying to become the first team to go 19–0 in a season. The Giants had narrowly lost to the Pats in Week 16. In the Big Game, New York held strong through three quarters and led 10–7 until New England scored with less than three minutes to go. Eli Manning and the offense responded with an unforgettable drive. On one play, Manning escaped what looked like a sure sack and threw a Hail Mary that receiver David Tyree *(right)* caught by trapping the ball against his helmet with one hand! Four plays later, Manning connected with Plaxico Burress for the winning score in the gargantuan upset.

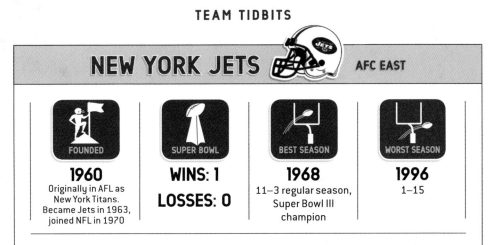

NEW YORK JETS

AFC EAST

FOUNDED	SUPER BOWL	BEST SEASON	WORST SEASON
1960	**WINS: 1**	**1968**	**1996**
Originally in AFL as New York Titans. Became Jets in 1963, joined NFL in 1970	**LOSSES: 0**	11–3 regular season, Super Bowl III champion	1–15

THE GREATS

Joe Namath, Quarterback With a personality as big as his game, Namath was a star inside and outside the football world. He was a four-time AFL All-Star, two-time AFL MVP (1968, 1969), and MVP of Super Bowl III.

Don Maynard, Wide Receiver This Hall of Famer was Namath's go-to target in the 1960s, made four AFL All-Star teams, and helped the Jets win Super Bowl III.

Curtis Martin, Running Back Signed away from rival New England, Martin had three Pro Bowl years with the Jets and won the 2004 rushing title.

Darrelle Revis, Cornerback The best shutdown corner of his era made four Pro Bowls in six seasons during his first stint with the Jets.

GOOD TO KNOW

Joe Namath was known not only for being a talented quarterback, but also for being cool and confident under pressure. After leading the Jets to an AFL title in 1968 and earning a trip to Super Bowl III, it was thought that Namath and his team would be chum for the mighty Baltimore Colts. (AFL teams were thought to be inferior, and the Colts were considered to be the greatest team in football history to that point.) During the lead-up to the game, a relaxed Namath (see Super Bowl week photo, *right*) famously told a heckler, "The Jets will win Sunday. I guarantee it." And he backed that statement up. The Jets pulled off one of the biggest upsets in football history, winning 16–7.

OAKLAND RAIDERS

AFC WEST

FOUNDED
1960
Originally in AFL, joined NFL in 1970. Moved to L.A. in 1982, back to Oakland in 1995

SUPER BOWL
WINS: 3
LOSSES: 2

BEST SEASON
1976
13–1 regular season, Super Bowl XI champion

WORST SEASON
1962
1–13

THE GREATS

John Madden, Coach This Hall of Famer led Oakland to the 1967 AFL title and a win in Super Bowl XI. He later became the world's most famous NFL commentator and helped establish the *Madden* video game series.

Jim Otto, Center The Hall of Fame anchor of the Raiders' line during the 1960s and early 1970s made nine AFL All-Star teams and three NFL Pro Bowls.

Al Davis, Owner–Coach Davis, the heart and soul of the Raiders, was a Hall of Fame executive who later became AFL commissioner before rejoining the team as owner and general manager from 1963 through 2010.

Jim Plunkett, Quarterback Plunkett led the Raiders to Super Bowl XV and XVIII titles despite starting the first season as a backup. He was the MVP of Super Bowl XV.

GOOD TO KNOW

The Raiders have the most recognizable fans in any sport. At each NFL stadium, fans do everything they can to give their team a home field advantage. In Oakland, that has included trying to terrify opposing players. Unofficially named the Black Hole, Raiders fans, particularly those who have sat behind one of the end zones at the Oakland Coliseum, have worn elaborate outfits with spikes and skulls and painted their faces in the style of the rock band KISS. Of course, in 2017, the Raiders announced their move to Las Vegas. Can the team recreate Raider Nation in Nevada?

PHILADELPHIA EAGLES

NFC EAST

FOUNDED	SUPER BOWL	BEST SEASON	WORST SEASON
1933	**WINS: 0** **LOSSES: 2**	**1949** 11–1 regular season, NFL champion	**1936** 1–11

THE GREATS

Chuck Bednarik, Center–Linebacker Football's last 60-minute man (someone who played offense, defense, and special teams) was a member of the NFL 75th Anniversary Team.

Reggie White, Defensive End After one season in the USFL, this fearless pass rusher spent his first eight NFL seasons with Philly. He made seven Pro Bowls, led the league in sacks twice (1987, 1988), and was the 1987 Defensive Player of the Year.

Steve Van Buren, Halfback Van Buren was one of the dominant players of the 1940s. The Hall of Famer won four rushing titles and led the NFL in rushing TDs four times.

Brian Dawkins, Safety Dawkins was the heart of the Eagles' defense in the 2000s. He made seven Pro Bowls with Philadelphia and was first-team All-Pro four times.

GOOD TO KNOW

He was nicknamed Concrete Charlie in part because of his off-season job as a concrete salesman. But the moniker also could have referred to the feeling opponents got when Chuck Bednarik hit them. He played each of his three positions at an All-Pro level during his career, from 1949 through 1962. He helped the Eagles to an NFL championship as a rookie. In 1960, he brought Philadelphia another title. It was Bednarik's tackle of Packers star Jim Taylor on the final play that ensured the Eagles' championship. The NFL may have seen players as good as Bednarik since his final game, but there's been no one as tough.

PITTSBURGH STEELERS

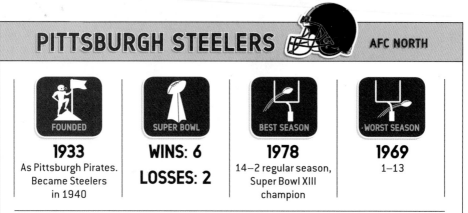

AFC NORTH

FOUNDED
1933
As Pittsburgh Pirates.
Became Steelers
in 1940

SUPER BOWL
WINS: 6
LOSSES: 2

BEST SEASON
1978
14–2 regular season,
Super Bowl XIII
champion

WORST SEASON
1969
1–13

THE GREATS

Joe Greene, Defensive Tackle "Mean" Joe Greene was a dominant defensive line force during the Steelers' 1970s dynasty. He was a two-time Defensive Player of the Year (1972, 1974), 10-time Pro Bowler, and four-time Super Bowl champion.

Terry Bradshaw, Quarterback The Hall of Fame QB was on four Super Bowl–winning teams, was twice named Super Bowl MVP, and was the 1978 NFL MVP.

Chuck Noll, Coach Noll took over a hapless franchise and coached for 23 seasons, winning four Super Bowls and 193 regular-season games with a 16–8 playoff record.

Jack Lambert, Linebacker This hard hitter with outstanding range in coverage made nine Pro Bowls from 1975 through 1983 and helped Pittsburgh win four Super Bowls.

GOOD TO KNOW

During the 1970s, the Steelers were football's dynasty. They won four Super Bowl titles behind a fierce defense known as the Steel Curtain. The team was loaded with stars (Hall of Famers "Mean" Joe Greene, Jack Ham, and Mel Blount among them), but the image and talent of Jack Lambert *(right)* defined those defenses. Famous for his missing front teeth, Lambert was a fierce hitter against the run. But he was also that rare athlete who could cover the middle of the field in Pittsburgh's Double Rotating Zone. That defense was the basis for the Tampa 2 schemes used in the NFL today, which often feature athletic linebackers in the Jack Lambert mold.

SAN FRANCISCO 49ERS

NFC WEST

**FOUNDED**	**SUPER BOWL**	**BEST SEASON**	**WORST SEASON**
1946 Joined NFL in 1950	**WINS: 5** **LOSSES: 1**	**1984** 15–1 regular season, Super Bowl XIX champion	**2004** 2–14

THE GREATS

Joe Montana, Quarterback The leader of the 49ers' 1980s dynasty was a two-time NFL MVP (1989, 1990), four-time Super Bowl champion, and three-time Super Bowl MVP.

Jerry Rice, Wide Receiver Rice, the greatest wideout in NFL history, was the all-time career leader in receptions (1,549), receiving yards (22,895), and touchdowns (208).

Steve Young, Quarterback This longtime backup became a two-time NFL MVP (1992, 1994). Young led the Niners to a win in Super Bowl XXIX and was a seven-time Pro Bowler.

Ronnie Lott, Safety Lott led the defense on four Super Bowl championship teams. He was a Hall of Famer and a member of NFL All-Decade teams for the 1980s and 1990s.

GOOD TO KNOW

Many consider Joe Montana to be the greatest quarterback in football history. The third-round pick led the 49ers to the Super Bowl in only his third year in the league. But as famous as Montana is for his success, he's just as well-known for his laid-back, calm demeanor when facing a challenge. Nicknamed Joe Cool, he threw the Catch to Dwight Clark, a famous last-minute TD to defeat the Cowboys in the 1981 NFC title game. He also led a 92-yard, last-minute charge to defeat the Bengals in Super Bowl XXIII. Moments before that pressure-filled drive began, he told a teammate that he had spotted comedic actor John Candy in the crowd.

SEATTLE SEAHAWKS  NFC WEST

FOUNDED	SUPER BOWL	BEST SEASON	WORST SEASON
1976	**WINS: 1** **LOSSES: 2**	**2013** 13–3 regular season, Super Bowl XLVIII champion	**1992** 2–14

THE GREATS

Steve Largent, Wide Receiver This Hall of Famer led the NFL in receiving yards twice (1979, 1985) and made the Pro Bowl seven times.

Walter Jones, Offensive Tackle Jones is considered one of the greatest linemen of all time. The Hall of Famer played all 12 seasons in Seattle and was a nine-time Pro Bowler and member of the NFL All-Decade Team for the 2000s.

Cortez Kennedy, Defensive Tackle The eight-time Pro Bowler spent all 11 seasons with the Seahawks, was the 1992 Defensive Player of the Year, and was a member of the NFL All-Decade Team for 1990s.

Richard Sherman, Cornerback This shutdown corner played receiver in college. He was a three-time first-team All-Pro (2012 through 2014) and helped win Super Bowl XLVIII.

GOOD TO KNOW

Acquired from Buffalo during the 2010 season, Marshawn Lynch carried the Seahawks while they searched for a franchise QB, rushing for more than 1,200 yards in each of his first four full seasons. But he will be remembered just as much for his unique Beast Mode personality. He famously snacked on Skittles to celebrate TDs (which led fans to throw Skittles on the field in celebration). He refused to speak to the media before the Seahawks' Super Bowl appearances. And when he announced his (first) retirement before the 2016 season, rather than hold a press conference, he Instagrammed a photo of shoes draped over a wire to indicate that he had hung up his cleats.

TAMPA BAY BUCCANEERS

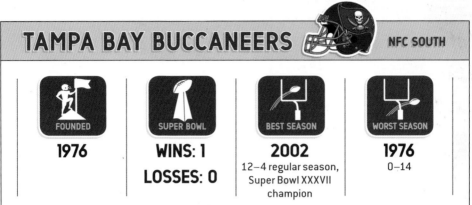

NFC SOUTH

FOUNDED	SUPER BOWL	BEST SEASON	WORST SEASON
1976	**WINS: 1** **LOSSES: 0**	**2002** 12–4 regular season, Super Bowl XXXVII champion	**1976** 0–14

THE GREATS

Derrick Brooks, Linebacker The leader of Tampa's dominant defenses of the 1990s and 2000s was an 11-time Pro Bowler and the 2002 NFL Defensive Player of the Year. Now in the Hall of Fame, he helped the Bucs to their only title, Super Bowl XXXVII.

Lee Roy Selmon, Defensive End This Hall of Fame pass rusher was the 1979 NFL Defensive Player of the Year and a six-time Pro Bowler.

Warren Sapp, Defensive Tackle A dominating interior pass rusher, Sapp was Defensive Player of the Year in 1999 and a member of the 1990s and 2000s NFL All-Decade teams.

Ronde Barber, Cornerback One of the top all-around corners of his era, Barber was a five-time Pro Bowler and a member of the 2000s NFL All-Decade Team.

GOOD TO KNOW

Talk about a rough start. The Bucs joined the NFL, along with the Seahawks, before the 1976 season. Seattle lost its first five games before getting the franchise's first win in 1976. The Bucs would go winless in their first season. And then they'd lose their first 12 games one season later. Wearing unique orange Creamsicle uniforms, the Bucs suffered some disappointing losses along the way. They were playing ugly football in 1977 and had been outscored 117–17 over a seven-game span before a trip to New Orleans. When everyone least expected it, the Bucs jumped out to a 26–0 lead on the Saints and won their first game ever.

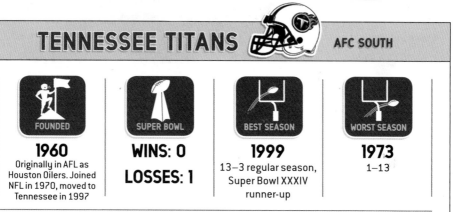

TENNESSEE TITANS
AFC SOUTH

FOUNDED	SUPER BOWL	BEST SEASON	WORST SEASON
1960	**WINS: 0**	**1999**	**1973**
Originally in AFL as Houston Oilers. Joined NFL in 1970, moved to Tennessee in 1997	**LOSSES: 1**	13–3 regular season, Super Bowl XXXIV runner-up	1–13

THE GREATS

Warren Moon, Quarterback The Hall of Famer skillfully ran the high-powered run-and-shoot offense in the 1980s and early 1990s. Moon led the league in passing yards in 1990 and 1991.

Bruce Matthews, Offensive Tackle He played all 19 seasons with the Oilers/Titans and made 14 Pro Bowls. His 296 career regular-season games is most all time among offensive linemen.

Earl Campbell, Running Back This bruising runner had a short career due to his physical style. He won NFL MVP in 1979 and three straight rushing titles from 1978 through 1980.

Steve McNair, Quarterback McNair became QB after the move from Houston to Tennessee. He was NFL MVP in 2003 and led the Titans to Super Bowl XXXIV.

GOOD TO KNOW

The Titans lost their only Super Bowl appearance in the most heartbreaking way possible. Facing the favored Rams in Super Bowl XXXIV, the Titans trailed 16–0 late in the third quarter when they mounted a comeback. With a little more than two minutes to go, the game was tied; then the Rams took the lead on a 73-yard TD pass. Steve McNair marched Tennessee to the Rams' 10-yard line with five seconds left and no timeouts. McNair found receiver Kevin Dyson *(right)* short of the end zone, and Rams linebacker Mike Jones tripped Dyson up as he reached for the tying score. The game ended right there, with the Titans coming up one yard short.

WASHINGTON REDSKINS

NFC EAST

FOUNDED

1932

As Boston Braves.
Boston Redskins
(1933–1936) moved to
Washington in 1937

SUPER BOWL

WINS: 3

LOSSES: 2

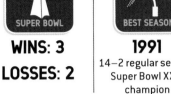
BEST SEASON

1991

14–2 regular season,
Super Bowl XXVI
champion

WORST SEASON

1961

1-12-1

THE GREATS

Sammy Baugh, Quarterback He was a pioneer under center as one of the first QBs to run a pass-happy offense. Baugh led Washington to two NFL titles (1937, 1942), led the league in passing four times (1937, 1940, 1947, 1948), and was a star defensive back and punter.

Joe Gibbs, Coach This legendary coach led Washington to three Super Bowl titles in the 1980s and early 1990s and was a two-time AP Coach of the Year (1982, 1983).

John Riggins, Running Back A punishing runner who led Washington's offense in the 1970s and 1980s, Riggins was MVP of Super Bowl XVII.

Darrell Green, Cornerback Green was one of the fastest players ever. He was a seven-time Pro Bowler who played 20 seasons in D.C. and was on two Super Bowl winners.

GOOD TO KNOW

For years, only white men played quarterback. Even if black players were QBs in college, many were discriminated against and asked to change positions once they got to the NFL, regardless of their talent and leadership ability. Washington's Doug Williams *(right)* helped change that. He had been in and out of the starting lineup during the 1987 season but was chosen by coach Joe Gibbs as the starter in the playoffs. When the Redskins made it to the Super Bowl, Williams became the first black QB to start a pro football title game. He tossed four TD passes in the second quarter of a 42–10 rout, threw for 340 yards, and was named game MVP.

TALK THE TALK

Call yourself a football fan? Then you need to sound like one! From *alligator arms* and *audibles* to *wishbones* and *zebras*, here are all the gridiron terms you need to know.

Alligator arms Imagine you're building a football team with species from across the animal kingdom: cheetahs, kangaroos, polar bears. (You have to be prepared for a playoff game in Green Bay, after all.) One animal that's not making the team: the alligator, who can't possibly catch the ball with those short arms. "Alligator arms" has become one of the greatest insults you can aim at an NFL pass catcher. It refers to when receivers, fearing a big hit, pull their arms back toward their bodies and protect themselves rather than reaching out to make the catch.
USE IT "I know that nasty hit really shook you up, but I need you to catch the ball, man. You can't get alligator arms when you go over the middle."

All-purpose yards A combined total of rushing yards, receiving yards, and all forms of return yards. Not to be confused with "yards from scrimmage," which is rushing and receiving yards only. Darren Sproles, then of the Saints, set the single-season record for all-purpose yards in 2011, with 2,696 (603 rushing, 710 receiving, 294 on punt returns, and 1,089 on kickoff returns).
USE IT "Can you believe how many all-purpose yards Sproles has? Rushing, receiving, returning—he's all over the field!"

Audible When the quarterback changes a play call at the line of scrimmage. For instance, maybe the original play call was a run, but after breaking the huddle, the QB sees the defense has stacked defenders close to the line of scrimmage. He is telling his teammates, "Nah, don't run that play, run this one instead." For some teams, an audible consists of the QB simply calling out a signal. For others (like future Hall of Famer Peyton Manning), calling an audible is a series of shouts, hand signals, and leg stomps that are better than anything you would see at a middle-school dance.

USE IT "I could totally tell that Aaron Rodgers was calling an audible. Did you see the way the players shifted after he started yelling?"

Ball hawk Just like the bird swooping down and snatching up a small woodland creature for its next meal, the ball hawk preys on an unsuspecting quarterback's pass. This term refers to a defensive player—almost always a member of the secondary—who has the sure hands and good timing to snatch away interceptions or wrestle the ball away for fumbles.

USE IT "That's Richard Sherman's eighth interception of the year! From now on, quarterbacks better pay attention to where this ball hawk is lined up."

Blind side When a righthanded quarterback is standing in the pocket, he throws with his left shoulder facing upfield. Out of the corner of his eye, the passer can typically see what's happening on the right side of his offensive line; after all, his chest is facing that way. But the left side, where his back is facing, is his blind side. (The right side is a lefthanded QB's blind side.) When it comes to pass protection, the left tackle is considered the most important player on the offensive line because he protects the blind side. He is responsible for keeping a speedy pass rusher from hitting his unsuspecting QB.

USE IT "Tom Brady never saw that sack coming, so he didn't protect the ball. The defensive end rushed the pocket from Brady's blind side."

Bootleg It's a handoff with everyone blocking left. No, wait, the quarterback still has it, and he's running out to the right, looking to throw it! That's a bootleg, a misdirection play on which the QB rolls to the opposite side of the play fake (usually looking to throw as his first choice).

USE IT "When Russell Wilson ran that bootleg, I didn't realize he still had the ball! Neither did the defense, which is why the Seahawks scored."

Bubble screen Sometimes you just want to get the ball into the hands of your best receiver right away. You want a bubble screen, a play in which the quarterback throws the ball immediately to a wideout, usually because the defensive back covering him will have a hard time making the tackle.
USE IT "The cornerback lined up 10 yards off Odell Beckham Jr. on third-and-three. Eli Manning threw a bubble screen, and the Giants had an easy first down."

Chain gang These are the guys on the sideline holding the down markers, one indicating the line of scrimmage on first down and the other the line to gain. The markers are attached by a chain that is 10 yards long. A third member of the crew marks the line of scrimmage before each play. There's also a crew on the opposite side of the field so that teams can look to either sideline to find the line to gain. In the event that a measurement is needed to determine whether or not a team gained a first down, one marker is placed at the first-down line of scrimmage. Then, the person holding the other end of the chain stretches it so officials can see whether the chain stretches past the ball. If it doesn't, it's a first down! And if it does . . . time to try again!
USE IT "On third-and-one, DeMarco Murray seemed to just squeak past the line of scrimmage. I can't tell if he made a first down, though. Here comes the chain gang, so we'll find out soon."

Checkdown For a quarterback, it's the last option. Almost every passing play in football has a short route built in. If nothing else is open, this receiver becomes the go-to option. It's not the most exciting play, and some QBs become too reliant on the checkdown. But it usually guarantees that the offense will get at least *something* out of a play.

USE IT "Philip Rivers wanted to go deep, but none of his receivers were open downfield. That's why he took the checkdown to running back Danny Woodhead for a four-yard gain."

Chop block A dirty phrase as far as defensive linemen are concerned. A chop block is when a defensive player is being blocked by one opponent and then a second offensive player comes in and blocks him at the thigh or lower. It is a 15-yard penalty to make that kind of high-low block. The rule was put in place because of the risk of knee, ankle, and foot injuries to unsuspecting defenders who were getting hit low by an opponent they couldn't see coming. Before the 2016 season, chop blocks were legal in some situations. Now you can only go low on a defender if it's a one-on-one situation. (The legal version is known as a cut block.)

USE IT "J.J. Watt was clearly locked up with the guard when the tight end came in and tried to take out his feet. The officials threw the flag, and the chop block will cost the offense 15 yards."

Coffin corner Some spooky stuff when it comes to the punting game. This is the corner where the sideline meets the front of the end zone, and some punters will try to kick the ball so that it crosses the sideline in the air as close to the front of that corner as possible. A properly executed coffin-corner punt will pin the opposing team deep in its own territory. However, if the kick crosses the goal line before it crosses the sideline (even in the air), it's a touchback. The slightest mishit will put the opponent safely out at the 20-yard line.

USE IT "Punter Dustin Colquitt was aiming for the coffin corner, and he nailed it. The Panthers will start this drive at their own four-yard line."

Dimeback No need to check the couch cushions for loose change. This is the sixth defensive back on the field for a defense. (The fifth is the nickelback.)
USE IT "The Steelers lined up with four wide receivers, so the Ravens countered by sending a dimeback onto the field."

Drag route Rather than run straight upfield, this is when a receiver runs straight across the field. It's a better idea than it sounds. The goal is for the receiver to escape the man covering him by running through an area of the field packed with bodies, then catching a short pass and turning upfield for a big gain.
USE IT "No wonder Rob Gronkowski lost his man while running that drag route—Gronk was so quick as he dodged in and out of traffic!"

Draw play A play-action pass, but in reverse! On this play, the quarterback drops back, poised as if he is going to scan the field and throw a pass. Instead, he hands the ball to a running back (or, in some cases, keeps it himself).
USE IT "On third-and-long, the defense was expecting the pass but was fooled when the Saints ran a draw play. First down!"

End around
The preferred play for a wide receiver who secretly wishes that he were a running back. On an end around, a player lined up at wideout or tight end runs behind the QB to take a handoff, then keeps going in the same direction, eventually trying to turn upfield.
USE IT "Speedy wide receiver Antonio Brown is the perfect player for an end around. He took that handoff and picked up 14 yards."

Encroachment Just a fancy way of saying offside. Specifically, this is when a defensive player crosses the line of scrimmage and makes contact with an offensive player before the ball is snapped.

USE IT "The linebacker was coming on the blitz, but his timing was off, and he ran right into an offensive lineman before the ball was snapped. Uh-oh! That's a five-yard penalty for encroachment."

Fair catch Returning a punt can be a dangerous job. You have to stand back and watch that high kick slowly sail toward you, all the while trying to figure out how you're going to avoid being crushed by the oncoming tacklers once you finally have the ball. Thus, the fair catch. This is when you see a return man on a punt (or, more rarely, on a kickoff) wave his hand over his head. It signals to the official and to opponents that he is not going to try to return the kick, so he can't be tackled. Defenders are penalized if they don't respect the fair catch.

USE IT "On an extra high punt by Dustin Colquitt, Devin Hester played it safe and signaled for a fair catch."

Flanker Some people mistakenly think any receiver can be called a flanker, but the term should only refer to a wideout who lines up behind the line of scrimmage. When you see a receiver who is lined up on the outside of the formation go in motion before the snap, that is almost always the flanker.

USE IT "Odell Beckham Jr. lined up as the flanker for the Giants, and when he went in motion, everyone on the defense reacted."

Flat That area right around the line of scrimmage, outside the offensive line. This is usually where you will find pass catchers who are not so fleet of foot.
USE IT "The tight end faked the block, then slipped out to the flat, where he was wide open for a short gain."

Flea–flicker A doggone exciting trick play. The running back takes a handoff from the quarterback, but before he gets to the line of scrimmage, he turns around and flips the ball back to the QB. Now it becomes a passing play! If it works right, it usually results in a big gain for the offense.

USE IT "The defensive backs came sprinting toward the line of scrimmage when they saw Todd Gurley with the ball. But Gurley flipped it back to quarterback Jared Goff, who had his choice of wide-open receivers downfield, a perfectly executed flea-flicker."

Forward progress This is all about how officials spot the ball at the end of a play. Unless the ballcarrier moves backward on his own, the spot of the ball is the farthest he moved it forward. Otherwise, a tackler could pick him up and run him backward five yards on every tackle.
USE IT "Matt Forte ended up on his backside on the 15, but he had made it all the way down to the 12 before he was hit. The officials will give him forward progress at that spot."

Gunner One of the toughest jobs in football. On a team that is punting, the gunners are the guys who line up outside and are supposed to be the first players downfield to make a tackle. They often face blocking double teams all the way down the field.

USE IT "The Titans were hoping for good field position, but the gunner got downfield and tackled the return man immediately."

Hail Mary

Football's version of a prayer. This play usually takes place at the end of a game or the first half. A team sends all of its receivers downfield, and the quarterback simply chucks the ball as far and as high as he can. It's a desperation play that rarely works out.

USE IT "The game was tied after a miracle play at the end of regulation. Aaron Rodgers's Hail Mary was tipped and then fell into the arms of Randall Cobb in the back of the end zone for a 55-yard touchdown."

Hands team

A very special part of a special teams unit. On a kickoff, these are the guys who are deployed when the receiving team expects an onside kick. Normally, the hands team is a mix of sure-handed pass catchers and nimble blockers. Typically, an onside kick is bounced high into the air. The front line of the hands team (those nimble blockers) will step up and try to prevent the opponents from reaching the ball, while the second line (the sure-handed pass catchers) is responsible for corralling the kick.

USE IT "The Chargers have pulled to within three points after that touchdown, and with only 30 seconds left, they'll try to recover an onside kick. The Chiefs will definitely send out the hands team now."

Hard count Defensive linemen just can't wait to get after the quarterback. They're eager. A quarterback can take advantage of this eagerness—and possibly get a free five yards—by using a hard count. This is when the QB, while calling signals at the line of scrimmage right before the snap, yells something particularly loud that sounds as if it would be the sign to snap the ball but isn't. The offensive line is in on the plan, but sometimes defensive linemen can be fooled.

USE IT "Matt Ryan drew the defense offside by barking out a hard count, and the five-yard penalty gave the Falcons a first down."

Hook and lateral The name for this trick play makes it sound simple: It's a hook route, followed by a lateral. But actually pulling it off is a bit more complicated. A hook route is when a receiver runs straight forward, then stops and turns around toward the quarterback. On this play, the receiver runs a hook; immediately after the catch, he laterals (throws a backward pass) to a teammate who is sprinting upfield. It takes perfect timing to make this play work. The hope is—with the defense moving to tackle the initial receiver—that the teammate will have nothing but open field ahead of him.

USE IT "Looking to spark the offense, the Texans went with the ol' hook and lateral. DeAndre Hopkins caught the pass 10 yards downfield, then immediately flipped the ball to a streaking Lamar Miller, who picked up another 30 yards. That play was just what Houston needed!"

Horse collar This is dangerous stuff, a type of tackle that is now outlawed in most cases. It's when a tackler grabs the ballcarrier by the inside collar of the back or side of the shoulder pads or jersey and pulls him down. This brand of tackling can cause major injuries. However, horse-collar tackles are still legal on quarterbacks in the pocket and ballcarriers within the tackles.

USE IT "The defensive back took the proper angle to cut off the runner, but he grabbed inside the shoulder pads and pulled him down from behind. That horse collar drew a flag and will add 15 yards to the end of the run."

Hot read The offense is at the line, and the defense is showing blitz. There are more pass rushers than the offensive line can handle. The quarterback might communicate to a running back or tight end to stay in and block. Or, the QB can go to his hot read. This is a receiver who will adjust his route so the quarterback can make a quick throw to a spot the defense will have a tough time reaching.

USE IT "T.Y. Hilton was the hot read on that play. The Texans brought extra blitzers, so Hilton ran a little slant route, Andrew Luck got him the ball, and Hilton had plenty of room to run."

I formation

This is a touch of old-school football that is still in use today. Think *power-running formation*. This is when you have a fullback, followed by a running back, in a straight line behind the quarterback. While a team can

fake the run with play-action, or use misdirection to fool the defense, the I is set up for the running back to churn out yardage with the fullback as his lead blocker.

USE IT "On second-and-two, the Saints lined up in an I formation with Drew Brees under center and Mark Ingram behind the fullback."

Illegal motion A five-yard penalty on the offense that can happen one of three ways: a player already set on the line of scrimmage goes into motion; a player off the line of scrimmage moves forward before the ball is snapped; or any player lines up but is not set for a minimum of one second.

USE IT "The Broncos rushed to the line, but Demaryius Thomas wasn't set before the ball was snapped. Denver will be flagged for illegal motion."

Icing the kicker A way of playing mind games with the opponent's kicker before a big kick. The opposing team will call a timeout and force the kicker to wait and hopefully make him overthink the upcoming kick. Coaches will often try to take the timeout right before the ball is snapped for that kick.

USE IT "Justin Tucker had a 48-yard field goal attempt to try to force overtime. The snap was made, but whistles sounded to stop the play before the kick was up. The Bengals had called timeout to try to ice the kicker."

Kickout block When done properly, it could mean a huge gain for the offense. A kickout block involves a blocker moving horizontally, rather than upfield. The goal is to find the defensive player farthest out on the edge and take him out of the play, opening up a running lane on the outside of the field.

USE IT "Kenneth Dixon bounced to the outside and picked up 25 yards on that run. The key was that kickout block by Marshal Yanda, which opened up a huge gap on the left side."

Lateral Another name for a backward pass. While only one forward pass can be thrown during a play (and that pass must be made from behind the line of scrimmage), a team may throw as many laterals as it wants over the course of a play.

USE IT "Trailing by five with only two seconds left, the Cowboys did anything they could to get into the end zone. After Dez Bryant made a catch, he threw a lateral to his teammate, who threw a lateral to *another* teammate, who lost the ball out-of-bounds."

Long snapper On a normal offensive play, the center is responsible for snapping the ball. Sometimes the quarterback is under center, which means the center simply hands the QB the ball. And sometimes the quarterback will stand three or five yards back, in a pistol or shotgun formation. It's different on field goal attempts and punts. On a field goal, the holder is often seven or eight yards away from the snapper, and the punter stands about 15 yards back. Timing is key for those special teams plays, and the snap has to be fast and accurate. That's where the long snapper comes in. Long-snapping is such a specialized skill that most teams carry a player whose only job is to make snaps on kicks and punts.

USE IT "Because of the torrential downpour, Stephen Gostkowski had a tougher kick than usual. But the long snapper delivered the ball on target to the holder, and Gostkowski's field goal split the uprights."

Max protect No, you don't need a quarterback named Max to use this strategy. Max is short for maximum. It's when an offense, expecting a blitz (or perhaps overwhelmed by a few star pass rushers), opts to keep eligible receivers, often anyone lined up at running back or tight end, in as extra blockers. It results in two or, sometimes, only one receiver going out on a route.

USE IT "Fearing the pass rush on that play, the Jaguars chose to go max protect to keep the heat off quarterback Blake Bortles. Allen Robinson and Allen Hurns were the only receivers Bortles had to choose from."

Muff Like a fumble, but not quite. A muff occurs on a change-of-possession play—a kickoff or a punt—when the return man loses the ball but never really had control of it in the first place. If the kicking team recovers a muffed punt, it gets possession but cannot return the ball.

USE IT "With the wind swirling, the Broncos' return man was never able to corral the punt. It hit off his chest and went through his arms—he muffed it! The ball bounced right to one of the Raiders."

Neutral zone

Neither the offensive nor the defensive side of the line of scrimmage. No player can line up in this area, which is approximately the length of a football and the width of the field.

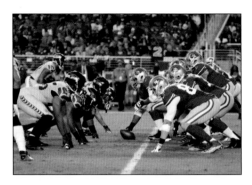

USE IT "He didn't jump before the snap, but the defender was lined up in the neutral zone. That penalty will cost the defense five yards."

Nickelback Not to be confused with the Canadian rock band, a nickelback is simply the fifth defensive back on the field. For a long time, it was standard for NFL offenses to play only two wide receivers at a time. Defenses countered with two cornerbacks and two safeties; thus, having four defensive backs was the most common setup for the D. When a third wide receiver entered the field, usually on obvious passing downs, defenses would sit a linebacker or defensive lineman and substitute a fifth defensive back. (And since a nickel is five cents. . . .) Of course, with most NFL offenses now playing three receivers on a regular basis, nickelback has become a crucial position for every defense.

USE IT "The Patriots opened up the game with three receivers, so the Broncos countered with three cornerbacks: starters Chris Harris Jr. and Aqib Talib, plus nickelback Bradley Roby."

Nosetackle The defensive lineman who lines up right over the nose of the ball. Sometimes called a noseguard, he is often the biggest player on the defense. He lines up directly across from the center, or just to the center's left or right, and is usually asked to wreak havoc on the middle of the offensive line. On running plays, the nosetackle aims to keep two or three blockers occupied so that his teammates have a better chance of getting to the ballcarrier.

USE IT "The Texans' inside linebackers relied on Vince Wilfork, a massive nosetackle in the middle of the defensive line, to keep opposing offensive linemen from paving the way for their running backs."

Pancake As sweet as it gets for an offensive lineman. This is when a blocker lands his block so perfectly that the defensive player lands on his backside. In other words, he gets flattened. Like a pancake. It isn't kept as an official statistic, but it is a point of pride for offensive linemen.

USE IT "The Cowboys love running this play behind Tyron Smith. He pancaked the linebacker on the outside."

Pick–six An interception (or "pick") that is run all the way back for a touchdown ("six," as in points). It's one of the biggest momentum swings a team can have over the course of a football game.

USE IT "Josh Norman read the quarterback's eyes perfectly, jumped in front of the receiver, and was off to the races for a pick-six."

Pistol formation

For years, a quarterback could receive the snap one of two ways. He could go under center (putting his hands under the center's butt and having the ball handed back to him), or he could stand five yards away and get

the ball flipped back to him in a shotgun formation. In the mid-2000s, the University of Nevada started a new trend with the pistol formation, which was a combination of the two. The QB stands three or four yards behind center to take the snap, with a running back aligned directly behind him.
USE IT "Robert Griffin III lined up in the pistol formation, forcing the defense to worry about the threat of a run on third-and-three."

Play–action A classic bit of trickery. This is when the QB holds the ball out like he's going to hand it off, then pulls it back and looks to throw instead.
USE IT "The linebackers bit on play-action, and that left Jordan Reed wide open in the middle of the field for a big gain."

Pocket A nice, safe place for the quarterback to be. At least, that's what the offense hopes. This is the area created when the offensive line drops back into pass protection. Ideally, it's a horseshoe-shaped ring of protection around the quarterback, who can scan the field and make his

throw without being touched by any defenders.
USE IT "The offensive line made sure Jay Cutler had plenty of time to stand in the pocket and deliver a strike to Alshon Jeffery for the first down."

Pooch Just like an adorable little dog you might call a pooch, this is an adorable little punt or kick. Well, maybe not adorable, but it's normally a short kick by design. The kicking team either wants to make sure a good return man doesn't get an opportunity or wants to pin an opponent deep in its own territory.
USE IT "With the always dangerous Devin Hester back to return, the Packers opted to pooch the punt, leaving the kick short but ensuring Hester wouldn't have a chance at returning the ball."

Post pattern This is a deep pattern designed to deliver a big play. The receiver sprints straight upfield before cutting toward the middle of the field at a 45-degree angle.
USE IT "Both safeties were cheating toward the sideline, so when Julio Jones faked outside and ran a post pattern, he ended up wide open in the middle of the field."

Prevent This is when the defense really wants to play it safe when protecting a late lead. The prevent (pronounced PRE-vent, with the emphasis on the first syllable) usually involves a lot of defensive backs on the field, all of whom are playing very deep zone coverage. The idea is to give up insignificant passing plays while not allowing a big one over the top.
USE IT "With a 10-point lead and only two minutes left in the game, the Jets went with a prevent D. They hoped to make the Dolphins settle for short plays that would run out the clock."

Pulling There's the bad kind of pulling, like what a player might do to his hamstring. But this is the good kind of pulling: when a blocker, instead of blocking the man directly in front of him, steps back from the line and runs to block a different defender. It adds an element of deception since the lead blocker comes from a different position than the defense would expect.
USE IT "Right guard Zack Martin was pulling on the play. He moved all the way out to the left edge, where he cleared the way for Ezekiel Elliott."

Quick kick A trick play that never really seems to bother the defense. This is when the quarterback, lining up as he would on a regular play, doesn't pass the ball or hand it off: He punts it. Teams usually employ the quick kick on third or fourth down. The idea is to catch the opponent off guard when there is no return man on the field, possibly allowing the ball to roll at the end of the kick.

USE IT "Ben Roethlisberger lined up in the shotgun on fourth-and-eight from the 35, but instead of running a play, he went with the quick kick. The Steelers downed the ball at the 10, which is where the Browns will start their next drive."

Red zone That imaginary area on the field between the opponent's goal line and the 20-yard line. Once in the red zone, the offense is in prime scoring territory. At this point, only a stout D, a turnover, or a missed field goal can disrupt a team's plan to score.

USE IT "The Eagles were in the red zone three times in the first half, but the Giants' defense came up big and held Philadelphia to field goals each time."

Rub A strategy used by NFL offenses to wipe a defender right out of a play. Basically, one receiver will run his route so that he crosses a teammate at some point. The idea is that a defender will either run into the other receiver or the defender covering the other receiver, allowing his man to become wide open. The trick is to do it so that it doesn't look intentional. If a receiver blocks one of the defenders while running his route, he will be penalized for offensive pass interference.

USE IT "Julian Edelman and Danny Amendola ran a shallow cross, creating a natural rub. With the cornerback taken out of the play, Edelman was freed up for a big gain."

Screen play A sort of misdirection play by the offense. This is a short pass in which the intended receiver already has blockers lining up in front of him. Often, on running back screens, offensive linemen will let the pass rushers sprint past them and move outside to set up their blocks. If the pass rushers take the bait, the play creates space and can lead to a huge offensive play. USE IT "The defensive linemen thought they had an easy sack, but the Packers were setting up a screen play for Eddie Lacy. He caught the short pass, and with three linemen in front of him, he had no problem picking up the first down."

Seam This is the imaginary line between the areas being covered by zone defenders. For instance, imagine a defense in which three defensive backs are playing zone. There would be two seams: one on either side of the defensive back playing in the middle. USE IT "Sometimes a speedy tight end can run up the seam and catch a pass that is just out of reach for both defenders."

Shotgun A formation that has been part of the game in some form as far back as the 1930s. This is when the quarterback, rather than going under center, stands about five yards back and has the center flip the snap back to him. The advantage is that the quarterback has a better view of the defense before the play and also doesn't have to worry about dropping back. While teams have found more ways to effectively run the ball out of the shotgun in recent years, it is typically a formation used with the passing game in mind. USE IT "On third-and-nine, Marcus Mariota set up in shotgun and called the play."

Slant A shorter route in which a receiver quickly turns inside and runs diagonally up the field. It's a route designed to beat a defensive back to the inside and potentially set up a long run after the catch. USE IT "At the snap, Dez Bryant faked outside and then ran a slant, leading to an easy pass for Dak Prescott."

Slot receiver The slot is the area between the end of the offensive line and the widest receiver on that side of the field. The pass catcher who lines up there is known as the slot receiver. It's a position in which a lot of smaller, quicker receivers such as Wes Welker have thrived over the years. And it can be especially tough for a defensive back to cover that man, since the slot receiver can run routes to either side of the field without having to worry about the sideline.

USE IT "Julian Edelman is especially dangerous as a slot receiver. He consistently shakes defensive backs by faking inside before cutting outside, or vice versa."

Sneak A play used in short-yardage situations. This is when the quarterback takes the snap from under center and immediately surges forward, hoping that his offensive linemen will push the defensive line back enough for him to gain a yard. Sometimes the QB simply finds a small crack in the defensive line and makes it through.

USE IT "Facing third-and-one, Joe Flacco went with the sneak and just barely picked up the first down."

Spy A popular way to counter quarterbacks who can beat defenses with their legs. Often, when facing a QB who is a running threat, the defense will assign a spy. This is a defender, usually a linebacker or a safety, responsible for shadowing the QB and being in position to stop him if he decides to run with the ball.

USE IT "Fearing Russell Wilson's mobility, the 49ers decided to use NaVorro Bowman as a spy to keep Wilson from breaking off a big run."

Squib kick Sometimes, especially at the end of a half or the end of a game, the only thing a team kicking off wants is to avoid giving up a touchdown. That's when the squib comes in. It's a shorter, bouncing kickoff that wreaks havoc with the returning team's setup. The kicking team gives up a little bit of field position, but it's often worth it if there are only a few seconds left.

USE IT "After taking a one-point lead with only six seconds on the clock, the Buccaneers opted for a squib kick to ensure they wouldn't give up a touchdown on the return."

Stiff arm Ballcarriers frequently absorb the biggest hits. But the stiff arm (sometimes called a straight arm) is their chance to strike back. Carrying the ball in one hand, the runner uses his other hand to deliver a blow to the potential tackler, hopefully knocking him down but at least warding him off for a moment. The statue for the Heisman Trophy, college football's most famous award, is stuck in a stiff-arm pose.

USE IT "Frank Gore delivered a stiff arm right to the chest of one defender, then rumbled for another five yards."

Stunt It's a much less exciting play than the name would suggest, but it can still be effective. A stunt involves teamwork between two pass rushers. One pushes straight ahead into the offensive line, requiring one or maybe even two blockers to stop him. Meanwhile, a teammate takes a roundabout route to the backfield, looping around his teammate. If all goes according to plan, that second defender will have a clear path to the quarterback.

USE IT "The offensive linemen held up against the initial push, but they were fooled when DeMarcus Ware looped around on a stunt and got the sack."

Sweep A running play in which blockers move swiftly to the outside to clear a path for a ballcarrier who travels horizontally before running upfield. The sweep was a go-to play for Vince Lombardi and the old Packers dynasties; Green Bay used nimble blockers to create easy yards in the rushing game.
USE IT "After running the ball inside for most of the game, the Bengals caught the defense off guard when they ran Jeremy Hill outside on a sweep."

Tackle box Are we talking about fishing? Nope, we're still talking football. The term is often used when discussing intentional grounding penalties. The definition is simple: It's the section behind the area between where the two offensive tackles line up.
USE IT "There was no flag for intentional grounding. Blake Bortles had scrambled left and was outside the tackle box when he threw it."

Tailback This is an old-school term for the position now known as running back. The tailback is the player who lines up farthest from the line of scrimmage in the offensive backfield.
USE IT "With an inexperienced quarterback but a strong offensive line, they're better off relying on their tailback and the running game."

Three-point stance It has nothing to do with a kicker's celebratory pose after a field goal. This is simply a common way offensive and defensive linemen get set before a play: with one hand on the ground. That one hand, plus two feet, equals a three-point stance.
USE IT "Khalil Mack sometimes stands up before rushing a passer, or he can act as a defensive lineman and start the play in a three-point stance."

Trap block Why would an offensive lineman let a defensive lineman simply blow past him into the backfield? If that O-lineman is setting up a trap block. An unsuspecting defender will get past the blocker in front of him with ease, only to find that he's run right into a trap! A different blocker will have looped back and will block that defender out of the play, opening up running room for a ballcarrier.

USE IT "The defender burst into the backfield but was taken out by a trap block. That's what opened up a big running lane for Carlos Hyde. Touchdown San Francisco!"

Trips Short for triples. This is a formation that involves three receivers lined up on the same side of the field.
USE IT "The Broncos went with four wide receivers for the third-down play. One lined up on the left side of the line, with trips on the right side."

Unbalanced line Normally, the offensive line has a center in the middle, then a guard and a tackle on each side. Every once in a while, though, an offense will change things up with an unbalanced line. Sometimes a team will send a sixth lineman into the game, putting three linemen on one side of the center and only two on the other. Or sometimes an offense will go with five linemen but align three on one side of the center and only one on the other.
USE IT "The offense went with an unbalanced line, putting three linemen on the left side of the formation. The defense expected the run to be to the right, but the misdirection play took it to the left."

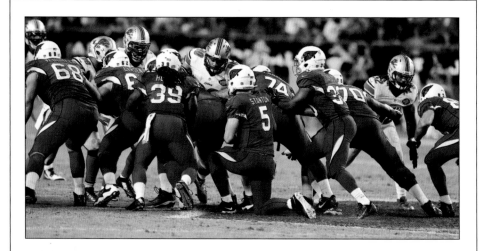

Victory formation When it's all over . . . except for a snap or two. Because of delay-of-game penalties, a team with the ball and a late lead cannot simply let the final seconds tick off without running plays. So instead of risking a fumble on a handoff to the running back, teams have the QB take the snap, then immediately take a knee to end the play, allowing another 40 seconds to run off the clock. The offense will often put a couple of players behind the QB, just in case something crazy happens, like a mishandling of the snap, which could lead to a fumble. That rarely happens, so when you see a victory formation, you know the game has likely been decided.

USE IT "The Lions were up by five with 53 seconds left, so they still had to run a play. We all knew that Matthew Stafford was going to come out in the victory formation."

Wheel route Many teams use a running back on wheel routes, but slot receivers can execute them too. It's a pattern in which the player starts by running toward the sideline, making the defense think he is running a short out route. But then he turns his shoulders and heads upfield on a deep route.

USE IT "With a slower linebacker trying to cover him, David Johnson ran a perfect wheel route, shaking the defender near the sideline before heading upfield."

Wishbone It's not used often in the modern, pass-happy game, but the wishbone was popular when power running offenses ruled football. This is a formation in which three players line up in the backfield behind the quarterback. One back is directly behind the QB, and the other two are a bit farther behind him and split to the sides. If you were to trace a line from the QB to the first back, then draw another two lines branching out from the first back to the other two, your drawing would resemble the wishbone you pull out of your Thanksgiving turkey.

USE IT "The Cowboys were so desperate to establish the run that they went old school and used the wishbone."

YAC Not an animal, but an acronym for Yards After Catch, a stat that counts only the yardage a pass catcher gains after he already has the ball.

USE IT "When it comes to YAC, no one has ever been better than Jerry Rice. The Hall of Famer regularly turned short passes into huge gains."

Zebras A nickname for the officials, in light of their black-and-white striped uniforms. An NFL crew is made up of seven on-field officials.

USE IT "The zebras played a big role in this game, as they called a combined 25 penalties."

PHOTO CREDITS

KICKOFF RJ Sangosti/The Denver Post/Getty Images (fans); G. Newman Lowrance/AP (field); John Iacono (King and Manning) **KNOW THESE NUMBERS** Stephen Dunn/Getty Images (Haley); Robert Beck (Brady throwing, Brady with trophy); Focus on Sport/Getty Images (Shula, Steelers Super Bowl XLIII, McKay); AP (Steelers Super Bowls IX, X, XIII, XIV); Jonathan Daniel/Getty Images (Steelers Super Bowl XL); Peter Read Miller (Rice); Bob Rosato (Manning); Robert Beck (Smith); Peter Read Miller (Dickerson); Tom Olmscheid/AP (Peterson); NFL Photos/AP (Flipper Anderson); Tom Dahlin/Getty Images (Patterson); Josh Umphrey/Getty Images (Cromartie); Neil Leifer (Dolphins); Andy Lyons/Getty Images (Harrison); AJ Mast/AP (Marshall: first, second, and fourth photos from left); Darron Cummings/AP (Marshall: third and fifth photos from left); Damian Strohmeyer (Strahan); Heinz Kluetmeier (Thomas, Favre); Brett Coomer/AP (Carr); Mitchell Layton/Getty Images (Morten Anderson); David E. Klutho (Rodgers); Doug Pensinger/Getty Images (Prater); John W. McDonough (Tomlinson); Al Tielemans (Moss); Harold P. Matosian/AP (Lane)

OBSCURE FACTS David E. Klutho (Lombardi Trophy, crate of footballs, James, Commissioner's Trophy, Stanley Cup); Greg Trott/AP (Sanders football); Focus on Sport/Getty Images (Sanders baseball, Young, Moseley, Howley); AP (Graham); Australian Scenics/Getty Images (cow); Bruce Bennett Studios/Getty Images (Mara); Courtesy Pro Football Hall of Fame (white football); Rob Tringali/Sportschrome/Getty Images (2009 Saints); spxChrome/Getty Images (floating money); mgkaya/Getty Images (pile of money); Mark Lennihan/AP (MetLife Stadium); Kelly Kline/Getty Images (Heisman Trophy); wellesenterprises/Getty Images (Green Bay sign); AP (Berwanger); Paul Hudson/Getty Images (stopwatch); Peter Read Miller (Eli Manning); Streeter Lecka/Getty Images (Peyton Manning); Tony Tomsic/Getty Images (Emmitt Smith rookie); Gene Lower/Getty Images (Emmitt Smith final); Christian Petersen/Getty Images (Lions fans); Kirby Lee/NFLPhotoLibrary/Getty Images (Browns helmet); Andrew D. Bernstein/NBAE/Getty Images (Larry O'Brien Trophy); Phillip Bartlett/Getty Images (grass and flowers); Peter Read Miller/AP (Montana); Focus on Sport/Getty Images (Blanda); Ron Vesely/Getty Images (Kelly); NFL Photos/AP (Unitas, Super Bowl I ticket); Peter Brouillet/Getty Images (Marino); Neil Leifer (Namath); Lisa Blumenfeld/Getty Images (McVay); Simon Bruty (Coughlin); Neil Leifer (Page); John Biever (Taylor); Focus on Sport/Getty Images (Howard); wavemoon/Getty Images (eagle); Michael Blann/Getty Images (yellow hard hat); F-M/Getty Images (bouncy ball); David Stluka/AP (Packers fans); Paul Sancya/AP (Favre); Paul Sakuma/AP (Rice); George Long (Blanda); Al Bello/Getty Images (huddle); Joe Robbins/Getty Images (Lions mascot); Jamie Sabau/Getty Images (Browns mascot); Wesley Hitt/Getty Images (Texans mascot); Rob Foldy/Getty Images (Jaguars mascot); Deanne Fitzmaurice (Super Bowl 50 field); Bob Rosato (Hester); Heinz Kluetmeier (Fog Bowl); Garrett Reid/USA Today Network (Super Bowl 50 ticket); NFL Photos/AP (AFL-NFL Championship ticket); RonTech2000/Getty Images (scoreboard with lights); Martin Ivanov/Getty Images (paintbrush with can); Dennis McColeman/Getty Images (sun); Lew Robertson/Getty Images (pizza); Hyrma/Getty Images (chips); Diana Miller/Getty Images (avocado with guacamole); Renee Comet/Getty Images (wings)

SKILLS TO MASTER John Leyba/The Denver Post/Getty Images (autograph); Christian Petersen/Getty Images (Fitzgerald); EyeEm/Getty Images (baby); Lauri Patterson/Getty Images (cubed cheese); koosen/Getty Images (bowl); Warren Price/Getty Images (chips with queso); Joe Robbins/Getty Images (punter); WesAbrams/Getty Images (garbage can); Rubberball/Getty Images (leaves); Brian Garfinkel/AP (keep the faith); Al Bello/Getty Images (Beckham Jr.)

THINK LIKE A COACH Mike McGinnis/Getty Images (Patriots coach); Greg Nelson (running game); Tom Szczerbowski/Getty Images (man blocking); Simon Bruty (zone blocking); John W. McDonough (protect the passer, get a move on); Hannah Foslien/Getty Images (extra help); John Cordes/AP (through the air); Ezra Shaw/Getty Images (West Coast); Dylan Buell/Getty Images (getting open); John Leyba/The Denver Post/Getty Images (get the QB); Evan Pinkus/AP (blitz); Leon Halip/Getty Images (twists and stunts); Jeff Siner/Charlotte Observer/MCT/Getty Images (stopping the run); Helen Richardson/The Denver Post/Getty Images (mind your gaps); NFL Game Pass (stack the box); Ricky Carioti/The Washington Post/Getty Images (coverage); Christian Petersen/Getty Images (press or play off); Tom Hauck/AP (play it safety); Michael J. LeBrecht II (kneeling QB); Al Tielemans (yelling QB); Hannah Foslien/Getty Images (pointing QB)

HE REMINDS ME OF . . . John Biever (Rodgers); Focus on Sport/Getty Images (Montana); Norm Hall/Getty Images (Johnson); John Swart/AP (Payton); Thomas B. Shea/Getty Images (Watt); Focus on Sport/Getty Images (White, Jim Brown); Christian Petersen/Getty Images (Patrick Peterson); Andrew Innerarity/AP (Sanders); Don Juan Moore/Getty Images (Miller); NFL/WireImage.com (Deacon Jones); Brad Rempel (Adrian Peterson); Norm Hall/Getty Images (Sherman); Michael Yada/Getty Images (Hayes); Stephen Brashear/AP (Thomas); Harry How/Getty Images (Reed); Paul Jasienski/AP (Kuechly); Tony Tomsic (Lambert); Al Pereira/New York Jets/Getty Images (Julio Jones); Tom DiPace (Moss); Dustin Bradford/Getty Images (Gronkowski); KHH/AP (Ditka); Ronald Martinez/Getty Images (Smith); Al Messerschmidt/AP (Muñoz); Al Bello/Getty Images (Beckham Jr.); Peter Read Miller (Rice)

TEAM TIDBITS Alexander Nicholson/Getty Images (helmet); Matt York/AP (Cardinals); John Biever (Falcons, Bears, Titans); Culture Club/Getty Images (Ravens); Amy Sancetta/AP (Bills); Simon Bruty (Panthers); Al Tielemans (Bengals); Damian Strohmeyer (Browns, Patriots, Broncos); Peter Read Miller (Cowboys); Sporting News and Rogers Photo Archive/Getty Images (Lions); Neil Leifer (Packers); Elizabeth McGarr McCue (Texans baby); Gregory Shamus/Getty Images (Texans helmet); Walter Iooss Jr. (Colts); John Iacono (Jaguars); Rich Clarkson (Chiefs); Al Messerschmidt (Chargers); Paramount Pictures/Everett Collection (Rams); Fred Kaplan (Dolphins); Rich Gabrielson/WireImage.com (Vikings); Bob Rosato (Saints); Heinz Kluetmeier (Giants, Titans); Walter Iooss Jr. (Jets); Damon Tarver/Cal Sport Media (Raiders); NFL Photos/AP (Eagles, Buccaneers); Tony Tomsic (Steelers); Tony Tomsic/WireImage.com (49ers); Jason Kempin/Getty Images (Seahawks); Andy Hayt (Redskins)

TALK THE TALK Al Tielemans (audible); Otto Greule Jr/Getty Images (ball hawk, zebras); James D. Smith/AP (chain gang); Harry How/Getty Images (fair catch); Leon Halip/Getty Images (Hail Mary); Brian Bahr/Getty Images (horse collar, long snapper); Tom Szczerbowski/Getty Images (I formation); Marcio Jose Sanchez/AP (neutral zone); Jed Jacobsohn/Getty Images (pick-six); Ric Tapia/AP (pistol formation); Al Tielemans (pocket); G. Newman Lowrance/AP (quick kick); Damian Strohmeyer/AP (slot receiver); Jeff Kowalsky/AFP/Getty Images (stiff arm); Tom DiPace (three-point stance); Steve Nehf/The Denver Post/Getty Images (trips); Norm Hall/Getty Images (victory formation)

BACK COVER Getty Images (blue finger); Valerie Loiseleux/Getty Images (red finger)